We spend a huge part of our lives talking, listening and responding to people around us. Yet ~~we think about what we're doing?~~ **It's as** good communication to 'just happen'. And ~~when it doesn't~~ happen – which is much of the time – our tendency is to blame the other person or simply accept that the conversation was somehow destined to fail.

There is another way. And that's to take personal responsibility for the quality of our conversations. If we put our minds to it we all have the power to influence every conversation for the better. Almost everything we do depends on conversation. It's how we plan and organise our lives. It's how we get close to people and build friendships. It's how we get to understand other people's points of view – and sometimes discover important things about ourselves. It's how we build our knowledge of the world. It's how we sort out problems, co-operate with one another, resolve conflicts and create new opportunities. In short, conversation is at the very heart of our lives.

The ability to carry on effective conversations is, in fact, the principal enabling skill of life. In other words, it lies behind just about every other life skill. If this is true, then surely it makes sense to be as good as we can at having conversations that work out for the best.

This book explains how to get more out of life by changing the way you relate to people through your everyday conversations. A lot of the anxieties, frustrations and 'people problems' we encounter as we go through life have their roots in poor communication. By getting better at how we understand and deal with other people, we can improve our lives in many different ways. As we hope you will discover, even a few small changes can make a big difference.

You don't have to read this book in one go, or try to put its ideas into practice all at once. If you like, keep the book with you. As you go through each day, try out some of the suggestions and see if they work for you. The ideas in this book are based on common sense and you may be familiar with some of them already. The goal is to build on your existing understanding of yourself and human nature, and become more conscious of what it takes to have satisfying, effective conversations.

The next two pages provide you with a guide to the contents of TalkWorks, which is divided into about 30 short sections. After you've been through the book for the first time, use the guide to refer back to the topics you want to read again.

A fresh look at conversation. Let's begin by taking a broad look at interpersonal communication. Why do some conversations work well while others fail? Why is misunderstanding so common? While nearly everyone agrees that the way we talk with each other is important, it's odd how little attention we normally devote to developing our talents at this vital activity. For example, it's possible to go all the way through the education system, from primary school to university, without receiving any training in effective face-to-face communication. The following seven sections prepare the way for the main part of the book, where we'll look in detail at the key skills behind rewarding conversations.

Good and bad conversations

Think of all the conversations you have in a typical day. They could involve people you know well, like friends and members of your family, or the colleagues you see every day at work. Or they could be with people you hardly know at all, like a shop assistant or someone you've just met at a party.

Some of these conversations go well. They're enjoyable and lead to a satisfactory conclusion. In short, they work. Others, however, go wrong. Some go around in circles or finish in an argument. Others die before they get going properly.

Most of us would like to have more conversations that go well. And that's a practical goal, because it's possible for everyone to get better at communicating.

There's nothing mysterious about improving your conversations. It's a question of learning some key skills and then making the effort to apply them. It's about recognising that conversations aren't predetermined, but can work out well or badly, depending on how you choose to behave.

We asked hundreds of people to tell us how they recognise good conversations. Time and again, people said things like this:

"Good conversations can really make a difference. Something useful or satisfying happens as a result."

"They feel like a genuine two-way experience, with both people equally involved and interested."

"The atmosphere encourages and supports the give-and-take of the conversation. So even if what's being discussed is difficult, the important things still get said."

"Both people feel they are being heard and understood. There's a willingness on both sides to be open and be influenced by what the other person has to say."

We call this kind of conversation a dialogue – and that's what this book is all about.

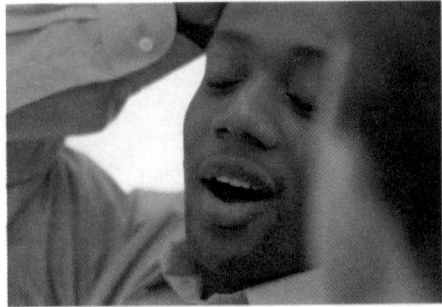

It's all about dialogue

To understand how to make a conversation a genuine two-way experience, think of communication in terms of dancing. When you dance with someone, you don't try and score points or 'win' in any way. Instead, you work as partners, responding carefully to each other's movements.

The idea is to co-operate rather than compete, so you both feel satisfied by the experience. In effect, you are both 'winners'.

It's just the same with a good conversation. You respond to each other. You help each other to perform well. You both get the opportunity to express your points of view, explain your needs and make your thoughts and feelings clear. It's about teamwork rather than looking out just for yourself.

An unsatisfactory conversation, on the other hand, feels more like a game of table tennis. The aim here is to score points, for one person to win at the other's expense. Conversations like this are about competing rather than co-operating.

A good conversation is a shared experience, a 'duet' rather than two solos that happen to coincide. It's like a 'jam' session where jazz players inspire and encourage each other as they create original music together.

To sum up, conversations work best when they are done as dialogue – when they are a partnership, with both people helping each other to make the most out of their time together.

Should every conversation be a dialogue?

When an air traffic controller needs to give an emergency order to the pilot of a plane about to crash, this is not the time for a dialogue.

On the other hand, take the case of Christine, the manager of a café who's giving orders to Dave, a new member of staff. She's doing it pleasantly, but nevertheless the conversation is basically one-way – a kind of lecture. If Christine is doing all the talking, then it's a monologue, not a dialogue. After listening to Christine for 20 minutes, Dave says: "I think I've got it." And then he gets on with his job. What a wasted opportunity!

Even when giving instructions or orders, making the conversation a dialogue can be very helpful to both people.

Suppose Christine and Dave turn their conversation into a dialogue, where they both contribute and are open with each other. Here are some of the good things that might happen:

Dave develops a much clearer understanding of what Christine expects of him because he's had the chance to ask several questions.

Dave also has the chance to offer Christine his own ideas: as a result he feels more involved and respected, and is therefore more likely to do a good job.

Dave and Christine strengthen their relationship: Christine gains a better understanding of what makes Dave 'tick' and this helps her work better with him in the future. Likewise, Dave ends up with a better 'feel' for what Christine is like as a person.

The point is that most conversations work out better if they take the form of a dialogue, with both people actively involved. Even when we're chatting just for the fun of it, the conversation will always be more enjoyable if people take turns and share the 'airtime'.

The two sides of effective dialogue

Think of conversation as an activity which has the aim of creating shared understanding. At any particular moment, one person is trying to be understood and the other person is trying to understand. Dialogue, then, involves two roles, both of which include talking and listening.

First, there is the role of the person who wants to be understood as he or she tells a story, communicates a message or explains a point of view. Let's call this role the 'Teller'.

When Jeff is talking to his wife about his experience at the doctor's surgery, he is in the Teller role. When Eileen is explaining to her son how she'd like him to keep his room tidy, she is in the Teller role.

The job of the Teller is to engage and hold the attention of the other person – and to make it as easy as possible for the other person to get the main points clear in his or her mind.

The other role in dialogue is played by the person who is absorbing the story, message or point of view. Let's call this role the 'Understander'.

The job of the Understander is to work hard at really understanding what the Teller is saying. This not only involves listening carefully, but also asking for more information and checking his or her understanding as the conversation goes along.

For example, Jeff's wife is in the Understander role as she listens to her husband and builds a picture in her mind of his experience at the surgery.

As you'll see later on, the skills of effective dialogue can be divided into two sets – one for the Teller role, the other for the Understander role.

Generally speaking, in good conversations people perform both roles, switching between being the Teller and Understander in order to help the conversation work out for the best. For instance, Eileen's son becomes the Teller when he responds to his mother and explains how he intends to sort out his room.

It can be very helpful for you to be aware of which role you are playing at any particular stage of a conversation. That's because conversations tend to fail when both people try to be the Teller at the same time. You can recognise situations like this quite easily.

It's as if the two people are having separate conversations. Rather than talking **with** each other, they are talking **at** each other. And so they end up talking **past** each other, with little real communication taking place.

If you feel this happening to you, try focusing on being the Understander for a while. Once you're convinced that you've understood the other person's point, then consider that you've earned the right to become the Teller for the next bit of the conversation.

In a good dialogue, people take care to share the airtime. So if you realise that you're dominating the conversation, take a break and invite the other person in. For instance, after describing his own visit to the surgery, Jeff might say to his wife: "You went to your doctor a couple of weeks ago. What was it like for you?"

On the other hand, if you're feeling left out of a conversation, invite yourself in, even if that means politely interrupting. Remember, everyone has an equal right to be heard and understood.

Don't misunderstand me, misunderstanding is normal

There are many enemies of effective conversation. We'll run across a number of them as we explore how to make conversations work well. But first, let's look at one of the commonest problems of all – misunderstanding.

Sarah tells Hugh that she won't be able to go to the engagement party for their mutual friend Deborah because she'll be away on a training course. Sarah regrets not being able to go, but that's the way things are. Later that week, Hugh talks to another friend, Carol, and mentions that Sarah has found "a way out of" going to the party, "or something like that". When Carol talks to Deborah, she mentions that she's "surprised" by Sarah's "attitude". Deborah is upset and hurt by the news.

When people talk with one another, what's the usual result? Full shared understanding? Or a large dose of misunderstanding? Unfortunately, studies show that misunderstanding is very common. It's all around us. The characters in the story about the engagement party are not bad people. They have simply allowed themselves to become caught up in a chain of misunderstanding.

What's behind a lot of our misunderstandings is our tendency to make assumptions or guesses about what's on another person's mind.

In many ways, we each occupy our own private world. These worlds may look much the same from the outside. But inside, they can be very different. We are all unique, with our own personal histories, beliefs, values and emotional patterns.

The fact is we can never fully know what's going on inside other people. We are not mind-readers. Instead, we have to rely on conversation to help us visit other people's worlds and have other people visit ours.

For this to happen with the minimum of misunderstanding, we need to be deliberately open **to** other people – and that means really hearing and understanding what they have to say. We also need to be deliberately open **with** other people – and that means actively sharing our own thoughts, feelings and experiences.

Sometimes, however, we act as if we can read other people's minds. This is what happens when instead of listening carefully we make guesses and assumptions about what people mean. All too often our guesses are incomplete or just plain wrong.

Sometimes we go astray because we assume that the other person is just like us – or at least a great deal like us. In this case, we are basing our understanding on our own view of the world rather than on what the other person is telling us.

At other times, we act as though other people are mind-readers. When we fail to provide other people with enough information about our situation and how we feel about it, we almost force them to make guesses and assumptions. And again, the result is often confusion and misunderstanding. So here are a couple of hints for better communication:

Don't assume that other people are just the same as you and that therefore you know more about them than you really do. Instead of guessing, make the effort to find out the facts for yourself.

On the other hand, don't assume that other people see you for the unique individual that you are – especially if you don't reveal much of yourself in your conversations. Instead of hinting and hoping, spell out exactly what you mean.

If you keep these two 'rules' in mind, you'll be less likely to misunderstand and be misunderstood.

Conversations that make a difference

To understand how to have conversations that make a positive difference, think for a moment about **why** we talk.

There's always a reason (or a combination of reasons) behind every conversation. If you know what's behind a conversation, you can avoid talking at cross-purposes – another big cause of poor communication. By understanding what the other person wants from a conversation, or indeed what **you** want from a conversation, you'll have a much better idea of how you can contribute to its success.

Let's think about some of the reasons why we talk with each other. People talk in order to share important experiences, get their points of view across and explain their needs. We use conversation to make plans for the future, solve problems and deal with conflicts. We talk with each other to relax and reduce anxiety, test out our ideas and build relationships. Through conversation we develop intimacy and open up new opportunities.

There are literally thousands of reasons for having conversations. What matters is that both people share the same purpose. If they don't, they'll end up talking at odds with each other.

Suppose Mary wants to tell you about her day at work as a way of unloading her anxiety. What she wants is for you to be a good listener and show some understanding. If instead you steer the conversation into a deep discussion about careers, offering all sorts of advice, you may well find yourself talking at cross-purposes.

If Dave wants to sort out the details of a trip with you, then reminiscing endlessly about last year's trip isn't going to move the conversation on.

Sometimes, it's useful to make the purpose of a conversation clear up front, especially if time is short. For example, you might say: "I'd like us to work out what we're doing at the weekend."

On the other hand, you can usually discover the purpose of a conversation with just a little thought. If Jason begins by saying: "This amazing thing happened at work today!" – then it's pretty obvious what he wants to tell you about. If Jill starts by saying softly: "About last night . . . I think I owe you an apology", it's clear she'd like to straighten things out.

If you're not clear what a conversation is about, spend a few moments thinking about it from the other person's perspective. Does she want me to act as a sounding board? Does he want me to help him think his way through a problem?

The main point is this. It's a good idea to understand why a conversation is taking place, whether it's you or the other person who has taken the lead. Knowing this, you'll be in a much better position to help the conversation fulfil its purpose.

While some conversations have an obvious purpose, a large amount of everyday communication falls under the heading of 'small talk'. That's not to say these conversations aren't important. Gossiping, chatting, joking, having a natter – they're all vital to keeping relationships alive. But again, they work best when both sides want the same thing from the conversation.

If one person simply wants to chat while the other is intent on having a serious discussion, the conversation is unlikely to work out well.

The skills of effective dialogue

It's time to move into the main part of the book. We're now going to look at the various skills that will enable you to become a more effective Teller and Understander.

Rather than describing all the Teller skills in one go, and then all the Understander skills, we'll discuss a couple of Teller skills and then a couple of related Understander skills. In this way, we'll be presenting the skills as a kind of dialogue, with the Teller and Understander taking turns.

We've divided the skills into four sets. Although the names aren't important in themselves, we've called the sets:

1 **Starting up**
2 **Getting connected**
3 **Staying on course**
4 **Moving on**

Always remember that in everyday life, these skills aren't applied individually but instead all flow together. They're easier to learn, however, if we look at them one by one.

The book also has several sections under the heading of **TalkWise**. In these sections, which are printed with a green background, we look at what might be called the 'wisdom' of better communication.

It's a bit like learning to drive. Being able to control a car isn't enough by itself. You also need to develop 'road sense'. Someone may be a very skilful driver, but can still cause accidents by his or her careless or inexperienced behaviour.

The **TalkWise** sections will help you develop your 'communication sense'.

As you work your way through the book, we hope you'll try out the ideas for yourself. You may well feel clumsy at first. This is only to be expected. Doing something different is always going to be awkward in the beginning. Remember the first time you tried to ride a bicycle or use a computer?

If all this sounds daunting, remember you already have many of these skills, at least to some degree. The aim is to help you become more aware of your good habits, so you can apply them more often. At the same time, by becoming more conscious of your negative habits, you'll be in a better position to avoid repeating them.

Starting up **Skills for Tellers** Suppose you tell Marcus about a difficult decision facing you at home. Out of curiosity, after the conversation has finished, you ask Marcus to tell you what he's learned from the conversation. As you listen to him, you are shocked to realise that Marcus hasn't really understood you at all. Who was responsible for the poor quality of understanding? Was it you, the Teller, or Marcus, the Understander? Even though mistakes might have been made on both sides, you have to take the main responsibility. Blaming other people for misunderstanding you is pointless. That would be like a teacher blaming a pupil for not understanding a lesson, or an author blaming the reader for not understanding a book. Let's begin by looking at two skills you as the Teller can apply early in a conversation to help promote better understanding.

Teller Skill 1 Engaging your partner's attention

"I think you'll see the problem in a different light if I tell you
what Jim wants."

How many times have you blamed someone else for 'not listening'? Probably quite often. In some cases, however, the blame may have been misplaced. Sometimes people don't listen because we are not providing them with something worth listening to. We may be so preoccupied with ourselves that we act as if the other person is there simply as an audience rather than as a partner in the conversation.

Good communicators, when in the Teller role, know how important it is to actively engage the other person's attention and get them involved in the conversation right from the start.

Put yourself in the Understander's shoes. Left on our own, our attention often turns inward. In effect, we talk to ourselves. We get lost in our thoughts. It can take quite an effort to redirect this attention towards someone else, especially if we already have some important things on our mind. This is why it's so essential for the Teller to 'hook' the Understander's attention at the beginning of a conversation.

Body language is important. It's vital to face the other person and establish eye contact. This is something we do automatically in particular circumstances.

For instance, we all know how to catch the eye of a shop assistant or waiter. The problem is we often forget to do the same thing in ordinary conversations.

How you open the conversation is particularly important. The good Teller knows that if the other person is to 'pay' attention, it helps to offer something in return. The following are examples of how you can do this.

Show how much you value the other person's attention: "Winston, I'd really like your opinion about . . ." or "Grace, I'd be grateful if you could help me sort out my thoughts on . . ."

Explain what the other person can get out of the conversation: "Danny, if we can sort out our plan now, I won't have to bother you with it again."

Use a bit of drama: "You'll never guess what happened to me here yesterday . . ."

If you anticipate that the other person is going to react negatively at the beginning of a conversation, it's worth preparing the ground with a few reassuring words.

For example, if Wayne wants to talk to his daughter Lucy about her poor school report, he could start off like this: "Lucy, I know you're already upset about your report, but don't worry. I'm not going to shout at you. I just want to see if there's any way I can help." After listening to this, Lucy is able to see the conversation in a more positive light. She's far more likely to pay attention and get involved in the conversation that follows.

If a conversation is going to be covering a lot of ground, it can be a good idea to offer the other person a 'map' of where the dialogue might go.

For example you might say: "I'd like to tell you about my ideas for the Club's Christmas party – and get your reaction to them. Nothing's finalised yet, so I'm open to suggestions. Then perhaps we can talk about who you think should be invited."

If you free someone from having to wonder about where a conversation is going, they'll be in a better position to devote their attention to the conversation itself.

Getting a person's attention is only the beginning. You also have to keep it. One of the easiest ways to lose someone's attention is to dump too much information, without giving the other person a chance to respond. So it's usually a good idea to deliver your points in bite-sized bits and provide your listener with plenty of breathing space.

Teller Skill 2 Using headlines and underlines to introduce key ideas, issues and topics "I'd like to tell you why I think you should apologise to your sister."

When you open a newspaper or magazine, what catches your attention is the headlines. Headlines are extremely useful because they tell you what the following article is all about.

It might be a news story: "Prime Minister Suffers Defeat In House Of Commons." It might be advice on health: "Lose 20lbs And Live Longer." Or it might be an opinion by a columnist: "Why I Believe The President Should Resign."

You can use the same kind of idea in your conversations to help focus the dialogue around specific topics, points and issues. If you have a firm idea of what you'd like to talk about, or what your main point is, make it clear to the other person by putting it in the form of a headline. Here are some examples:

Carol is telling her friend about her day at work. Her headline is: "The entire day was one disaster after another." She goes on to tell her story in more detail, having first made sure that her friend gets the overall point.

Michael is talking to his wife, Sandra, about their son. He says: "I've just found out that Alan has won the school prize for a drawing he's done. Maybe we should talk seriously about his artistic talent."

They go on to have a discussion about their son's artistic potential, their reactions to it and how they can help Alan plan his future. The discussion is a development of Michael's headline.

So if you know what your topic, main point, subject or theme is, say it up front. That way, you'll give the other person a good idea of how to make sense of what follows and how he or she can best contribute to the conversation. A headline helps in the same way that the picture on a jigsaw box helps someone fit the puzzle together.

To be able to use headlines, it's a good idea to think ahead a little. Pause for thought and ask yourself: "What is it that I really want to talk about?" or "What is the big point that I want to get across?" Having worked this out, give it straight to the other person.

If you merely hint about a topic or issue, and don't bring it into the open, then you shouldn't be surprised if the conversation doesn't move in the direction you want. This up-front way of talking is especially important if the issue is in any way serious or significant.

Suppose you want to talk with a friend on the phone about going on a cycling trip. You call and get her answering machine, which gives you 15 seconds to leave a message. To make sure your friend understands what you want to talk about (and calls you back), you might say: "You know that cycling trip we keep promising ourselves? Well, I'm free next weekend and I've got a great idea about where we could go. Let's talk about it." That's another example of a headline.

Here are some more:

Adrian is talking to Jenny, his colleague at work. He says: "I'd like to tell you what I thought about your ideas for changing our computer system. There were a few points that concerned me, but overall I really liked your proposal. Let me tell you what I particularly liked." This headline gives Jenny plenty of clues about how to make sense of the conversation that follows.

Amy is talking to her mother. She says: "Mum, I know you're worried about me staying out late, but I have a plan I think you'll agree with." The headline gives Amy's mother a clear steer on what the focus of the conversation is going to be. She may still be worried, but she's more likely to listen with a positive frame of mind.

Headlines can be used with stories. Jay is talking with a friend about a recent trip abroad. He says: "What really surprised me about Greece was just how different the people were to what I expected. Time and again, I found myself having to throw my old ideas away."

Jay has set the stage for the conversation by putting his theme at the beginning.

Headlines can be used with messages. Lillian is talking with her husband Larry about a medical issue. She begins by saying: "Larry, I've decided not to go ahead with the treatment. We both know it's not going to work. It's just postponing the inevitable and I don't want to subject myself to more misery."

Lillian starts with a strong headline. She and Larry go on to have a serious discussion about the future.

Headlines are also useful when you want to share a point of view. Nicholas and his brother Jonathan are talking about work. Early in the conversation, Nicholas says: "I believe everyone should have the right to strike if they think they're not being paid properly for their job."

Nicholas has put his cards on the table, and the brothers go on to explore each other's opinions in greater depth.

You can use headlines throughout a conversation to introduce new topics and ideas and keep the dialogue focused as it develops. They can act as conversational 'stepping stones'. There will be times, however, when an issue only becomes clear as you go along. As you talk, suddenly, the penny drops. Rather than keeping this thought to yourself, say it out loud, as if you are underlining a key sentence in a book. We can think of these statements as 'underlines'.

Underlines act as a kind of delayed headline, and often take the form of a mini summary. Here are some examples:

Timothy is talking to his girlfriend Angie about a trip they are planning. He is obviously fumbling a bit. Then the light goes on and he says: "Now I realise what's bothering me. I am looking forward to the trip, even though I might not sound very enthusiastic. But the thing is – I'm worried about how much it's going to cost. I'm not sure it's what we should be doing with our money." Now that the concern has been made clear through an underline, Timothy and Angie can work on dealing with it.

David is talking about an important meeting. After describing various incidents, he sums up with an underline: "All in all, I was pleased with the way I handled myself."

Hilary is talking somewhat vaguely to her friend Evelyn about her teenage son's social life. After a while, a thought strikes her and she says: "Now that we've been talking about this for a bit, it's become clear that what troubles me the most is John's choice of friends." This underline helps to focus the conversation and lead it into exploring some solutions.

Here's a situation you might well recognise. Charlie and Fred are at a loose end on a Sunday afternoon. They chat but the conversation is rather aimless. After a while, they drift off to the cinema. Neither enjoys the film. In fact, they have a terrible time.

Afterwards, Charlie tells Fred that he never wanted to go to the cinema in the first place. Fred is amazed. He didn't want to go either but had assumed that Charlie did.

What had gone wrong? Neither of them had taken the step of raising the issue that was on both their minds. Because the issue remained hidden, it wasn't discussed and both people ended up making false assumptions.

This problem would not have happened if one of them had formed a headline to bring the conversation into focus: "I don't want to waste the afternoon, so let's talk about the options. I have a couple of suggestions to make, and I'm sure you have ideas as well."

Starting up Skills for Understanders One of the most important qualities of the effective Understander is patience. Good Understanders are willing to provide the other person with the necessary time, attention and encouragement to get their points across. Simply slowing down and giving yourself more time to consider what the other person is saying can really help improve the quality of your understanding. We'll now look at two basic skills you can use to help you become a more effective Understander.

Understander Skill 1 Visibly tuning in to your partner

If you've ever driven a car, you will know what it's like to be on autopilot. As you drive along, you're hardly aware of the passing scenery. Suddenly, your attention returns to driving and you realise that miles have passed by without your noticing.

A similar experience can easily happen in a conversation if you fail to 'tune in' consciously to the other person. At best, you're only half involved. You go through the motions, but you're not really there.

The good Understander works hard to focus on the other person and the story, message or point of view he or she is conveying.

It's like tuning in a radio. The trick is to get rid of interference and 'lock on' to what the other person is saying. In conversations, 'noise' can come from many different sources. As you listen, you might be distracted by the surroundings. The place is busy and you find it hard to focus. Or the noise might be inside your own head. You can't stop thinking about an argument you had earlier in the day.

So, the challenge is to clear your own mind as much as possible to make room for the other person's words. If the issue being discussed has any importance at all, put the newspaper down, turn off the TV, cut the volume on the hi-fi and create space in your mind for what you are about to hear.

It's vitally important that the other person is aware of your attention. This is the vital first step towards encouraging someone to express himself or herself. **Be visibly tuned in.** People read your body language. They can tell if you are paying attention to them or not.

Here are some tips on how to demonstrate that you're tuned in and interested in the other person:

Face towards your conversational partner. Let the 'attitude' of your body say to the other person: "I'm here, I'm with you, I'm listening."

Be relaxed and open, rather than stiff or hunched up. Don't send signals that distract the other person from your "I'm listening" posture. Maintain eye contact at a comfortable level, but don't stare.

Use your facial expressions to show you're in tune with the mood and messages of the other person. So, if the other person is being serious, show your understanding by looking serious yourself. Be genuine, however. No one wants an actor or a clown.

Use gestures to indicate you are in touch. For instance, nod from time to time. It's a simple thing to do, but is perhaps the easiest way to show that your receiver is switched on. Or use some other gesture like leaning forward to show that you are paying extra attention to a particularly important point.

Watch two people deeply engaged in a conversation. They do all these things, but they do them naturally. If you are genuinely interested in the other person, your gestures will be natural as well.

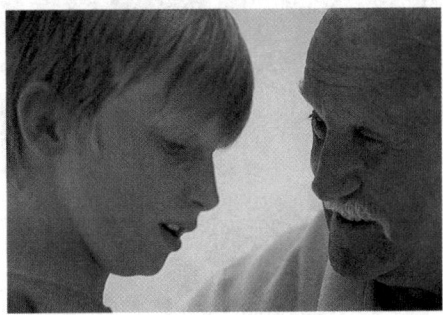

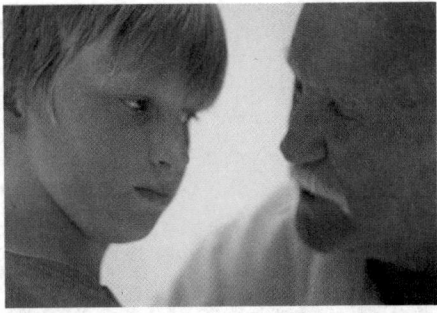

Understander Skill 2 Listening actively with an open mind

Effective listening is not a state of mind, like being happy or relaxed. It's not something that 'just happens'. The first thing to realise about listening is that it takes work to listen well, just like it takes work to do mental maths or recall a memory. Good Understanders are active rather than passive listeners.

There are two other important things to know about effective listening. One is the need to listen with an open mind – in other words, with an attitude that says: "I'm listening in order to learn." If you fail to approach a conversation as a 'learner', you won't really be listening. Second, it's important to listen not only to spoken messages but also to the unspoken signals sent out by the other person – through his or her body language, for example.

Listening to spoken messages.
Listening with an open mind means listening without distorting what the other person is saying, even though you might not like what is being said.

We all have opinions on just about everything. So when we're listening, it's tempting to judge what we're hearing from our own perspective. We say things to ourselves like: "Why did he do that? That was silly. I wouldn't have done it that way."

With open-minded listening, you avoid jumping to conclusions, making snap decisions or anticipating what you think you're going to hear. How many times have you made up your mind about the other person's point even before it's been fully delivered? That's not open-minded listening.

George, in the Teller role, is talking to a friend about his relationship with his wife. He says: "She's left me, but she keeps 'returning' in little ways . . . You know, she calls to ask questions about possible divorce proceedings. Then she wants to meet for a drink to discuss what to me are trivial issues. It's like she's playing with me . . . I don't know."

If Anne listens to George with a closed mind, this is what might go on inside her head: "There goes George again, feeling sorry for himself. When is he going to get over it?" Rather than focusing on George, Anne is listening more to her own reaction than to what he is actually saying.

If Anne listens with an open mind, she might say something quite different to herself: "George seems confused about his wife's behaviour. He's probably wondering what her 'game' might be." This time, Anne has concentrated directly on George's message.

There are many enemies to the kind of listening needed for good dialogue. Here are some of them. (Do you recognise any of yourself in the descriptions?)

Pretend listening. We appear to be listening, but we're not. We may be hearing the words, but we're not working to discover what they mean. When the Teller catches us and says: "You're not listening", we might reply, "Yes I am. I can repeat every word you've said." Not surprisingly, this reply does not satisfy the Teller. Listening is more than being a tape recorder.

Judgmental listening. We listen in order to determine whether what the Teller is saying is right or wrong – in our opinion. Joanna 'listens' to Rupert and thinks: "What a crazy thing to do."

Superficial listening. We listen only on the surface and five minutes later we can't remember what's been said. Similarly, we listen only to the things we want to hear – blocking out the points that make us uncomfortable, for example.

Distorted listening. We listen through distorting filters, such as personal prejudices and stereotyping. For instance, when the Teller is talking about a friend who has joined a particular religious group, the Understander instantly takes a negative view because he 'knows' what 'they' are like. Another example: Linda has been jobless for some time. The Understander dismisses her as a 'loser' and fails to hear her interesting observations.

Past behaviour-based listening. We assume that the person you are listening to is always the same. We do not allow for change. For instance, knowing George, we expect that everything he says will be tinged with self-pity. So we hear self-pity even when he is trying to break free from this behaviour.

Attraction-based listening. The Understander believes that what the person is saying is as attractive (or unattractive) as the person saying it. Paul is attractive, so his ideas always sound good to you. Edna is not attractive: her ideas never sound as good.

Jumping-ahead listening. We anticipate what the other person is going to say and 'listen' to this instead of sticking to what is actually being said. Similarly we 'hear' things that exist only in our imagination. When Hussein says to Frank: "Sorry, but I can't give you a lift tomorrow", Frank imagines that Hussein is angry with him for some reason and builds a whole story in his mind around this invented fact.

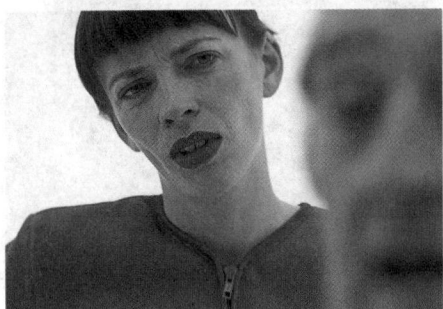

How you listen to someone greatly influences how you respond to them. You may seem to be listening carefully, but your responses will give you away.

Open-minded listening is not the same as internally approving of what the other person is saying. You can listen openly to Ian's ideas about politics without approving of his point of view. If you listen with an open mind, you suspend your judgement and always allow for the possibility of learning something.

If you've made up your mind before the conversation takes place, and if you are not willing to be influenced by what you hear, then no real communication can happen.

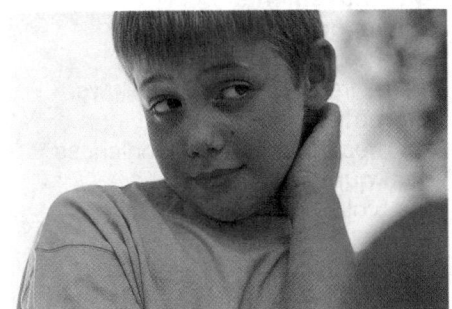

Listening to non-verbal messages.
Not all of your conversational partners' messages are verbal (spoken). We all send non-verbal (unspoken) signals or messages as well. These often add colour to what we say in words. Sometimes they even completely change our verbal message.

When you are in the role of the Understander, the trick is to 'read' these non-verbal messages but without making too much of them. The face and body are extremely communicative. Here are some of the ways that non-verbal signals can give a particular spin to our spoken messages:

Body movements
Posture, gestures.
Facial expressions
Smiles, frowns, raised eyebrows.
Automatic responses
Fast breathing, blushing, paleness.
Vocal qualities
Tone, volume, speed, pauses, silence.

David says to Jennie: "I hope you don't mind my taking up your time like this." Jennie replies: "No, I don't mind at all." But she hesitates before she responds, frowns and takes a quick peek at her watch. What was her real answer? A person's non-verbal behaviour has a way of 'leaking' messages to others.

Our non-verbal behaviour often modifies our verbal messages in the same way that emboldening words or adding exclamation marks gives extra meaning to written language.

Non-verbal behaviour can **confirm** what is being said verbally. For example, when Constance replies: "That's right!" her eyes light up, she leans forward a bit, and she speaks very animatedly. Her non-verbal behaviour clearly confirms her verbal message.

Non-verbal behaviour can also **emphasise** what is being said. When Joe says: "You're wrong! I don't want that job!" and looks you right in the eye and pounds the table, it's obvious that he means what he's saying. Non-verbal clues often add emotional colour or intensity to verbal messages.

On the other hand, non-verbal behaviour can also **contradict** or **confuse** what is being said verbally. When Rebecca challenges Barry about his rude behaviour, he denies that he's upset, but his voice wavers and he blushes. His non-verbal behaviour probably carries the real message.

A word of warning. Be careful about reading too much significance into non-verbal behaviour. We listen in order to understand our conversational partners rather than to play at being a psychologist. So it's a good idea not to focus too much on this or that bit of non-verbal behaviour. A frown, for instance, can be a sign of concentration as well as confusion or disapproval. Rather than jumping to conclusions, take a few moments to consider and confirm your hunches. While concentrating too much on someone's folded arms, tight lips or half-smile, you might miss the main point being said.

TalkWise
Creating the right climate for good conversations

Think of a conversation as a kind of plant. Plants need a supportive climate in which to take root and flourish. So do conversations.

We asked a group of people to describe the conditions they associate with conversations that go wrong in some way. Here are a few of the things they mentioned:

Not being paid attention, being pressured or put under attack. Being patronised or put down, having feelings ignored or dismissed. Being lectured at or receiving unwanted advice, not having the chance to have a fair say.

There's a simple rule that can help us avoid damaging or killing conversations through negative conditions of this kind. It's at least as old as the Bible: **treat other people in the way you want to be treated yourself.**

If you don't like being threatened, for instance, then it's only fair not to threaten other people. This is a very practical approach because people tend to mirror each other's behaviour. For example, if you pay a lot of attention to someone, he or she will tend to give you the same level of attention in return.

Let's take a closer look at how you can help create the right conditions for conversations to flourish:

Base your conversations on mutual respect. Our need to communicate runs from chats with shop assistants to complex discussions with family members, friends, teachers, doctors and people at work. All these conversations go better if they are based on respect. It's when people feel disrespected and undervalued that many of the problems begin.

While all people are worthy of respect, there are different degrees. At the lower end of the scale, respect is shown as civility and politeness. At the other extreme, respect takes the form of love and devotion.

Clearly, it doesn't make sense to treat everybody with love and devotion, but being civil is the minimum standard necessary for good conversation. We all know what constitutes being polite, and we all know that we like to be treated this way ourselves. Yet how many conversations are ruined by the absence of even basic politeness?

Consider all those people who play a role in your life but are not family or close friends. There are the people who serve you in the burger bar, who sell you tickets for the bus or train, who come to fix the washing machine and so on. You might not become firm friends with any of them, but they deserve your respect just as you deserve theirs.

Don't play power games.
Conversations go better when they are 'on the level' – in other words, when one person isn't talking down to the other. Even when the two people are not equal in some way – say a headteacher talking to a pupil, or a manager talking to an office junior – the conversation works best when this difference in status is not emphasised.

People who like to feel more 'important' than the other person don't make good conversationalists. They tend to dominate the conversation, making it more or less one-way communication.

It's easy to slip into playing this power game, so from time to time ask yourself – am I treating the other person how I'd like to be treated in his or her position?

Remember, taking turns is at the heart of dialogue. The turns don't have to be exactly equal. But both people need to recognise that the other person always has a right to his or her share of conversational air time.

Take responsibility for the success of the conversation. It's not fair for one person in a conversation to think: "It's the other person's job to make this exchange interesting and worthwhile. Sure, I'll talk with her, but she has to take the initiative, share her ideas and feelings, and do all the work."

That's like being in a boat with a friend and expecting her to do all the rowing. (You wouldn't be surprised if your friend gave up rowing altogether. Or even pushed you overboard.)

Conversations like this seldom work well. Both people in a conversation need to be actively involved, sharing their thoughts and feelings, responding to each other, looking for ways to move the conversation forward.

When a conversation seems to be running into problems, both people need to make it their responsibility to get it back on track.

It's no good just blaming the other person for a breakdown in communication and leaving it at that. There are nearly always things you can do to repair a conversation. (See page 120 onwards for ideas on how to fix conversations that are in danger of failing.)

Aim for a win-win result. Some conversations – like school debates – are deliberate competitions, where the aim is to produce a winner and a loser. But most conversations work out better if both sides win in some way. At the very least, this means both people having the chance to air their views and be understood. Setting out to 'beat' your partner in a conversation – for instance, by trying to make him or her feel small – does not create a supportive climate for dialogue.

Stay open to change. If you enter a conversation with your mind already made up about the outcome, don't be surprised if your conversational partner soon becomes frustrated.

When the other person realises that you are unwilling to change your mind as a result of what is being said, no matter how important or valid it is, the conversation can easily fall apart or turn into a confrontation.

Treat every conversation as an opportunity to learn something new and develop fresh ideas.

Getting connected **Skills for Tellers**

What happens when your friend Yvonne listens to you talk? As she tries to piece your points and messages together, she wonders: "What does it all really mean?" If you're sending out messages that are hard to make sense of – for example, by being vague or fuzzy – here's what can easily happen. As Yvonne struggles to understand you, she has to concentrate on what you've just been saying and therefore misses some of what you're saying now. So she gets more and more lost. And then when it all becomes too much effort, she gives up and lets her attention drift elsewhere. Good Tellers do what they can to make their meaning crystal clear. Here are two simple ways you can make it easy for the other person to hear and absorb your points.

"First, let me tell you who was there and how the whole thing started."

When you are in the Teller role, your story, message or point of view will be better understood by your conversational partner if you provide some background or context for what you are saying.

Too often, we launch right into the middle of things, sowing the seeds of confusion rather than preparing the Understander for the conversation that follows. The Understander struggles to make sense of what you're saying and probably makes some false assumptions. The impact of the story, message or point of view is lost in the confusion.

We can learn a lesson from film directors, who are experts at preparing the viewer for the film that follows. They use the opening section of a movie to set up the story they are going to tell. After a shot or two to grab your attention, the next few scenes provide you with the background for the story and introduce you to the main characters. Good directors, in other words, are skilled at putting you in the picture.

When you're setting up your story, preparing your message or formulating your point of view, think about what's already inside the mind of the Understander. Ask yourself: "What can I safely assume the other person already knows?" Or to put it another way: "What can I say that will help the other person understand what we're about to discuss? Is she aware of the background to the situation I want to talk about? Does she know the people I'm going to be mentioning?"

The good Teller, when telling a story, sets the scene in the other person's mind by first covering the basics such as who, what, where, when and why. Let's consider some examples:

Douglas is talking with Maria about a problem with his computer. He sets up the story by saying: "I've had my computer for nearly three years and now it's packed in. I bought it from a shop that's gone out of business, so I can't get any help there. This bloke called Ray, who used to work in the shop, said he could fix it, but I can't get hold of him. And the thing is, I've got a load of work to do by the end of the week." Now that Maria understands the background to Douglas's situation, the conversation can get under way.

The aim is to paint enough of the picture for the other person to begin to 'be there' with you.

It's easy to start off a story part way through without even realising it. For instance, if you've been mulling something over for a while before you talk about it, it's tempting to begin the story at the point where you left it in your mind.

If you want to get a message across clearly, again it's helpful to provide some background:

Kate is a head teacher, talking to the school's caretaker. She says: "I've had quite a few phone calls from parents who're worried about security in the school – you know, strangers wandering about the place. I think it's important we keep the gates locked during the day. So I'd like you to provide me with a list of exactly who has keys."

By taking the trouble to explain what's behind her request, Kate ensures that the importance of her message is clear to the caretaker. And by knowing something about the background, the caretaker is also in a position to add his own ideas about how the school could improve its security.

Providing context can also be useful when you are sharing your point of view:

Rod is at a meeting in the community centre. The issue is whether to allow a group of people with AIDS to use the centre for its meetings. He says: "You all know how worried I've been about this. However, I've been talking with some of the doctors at the hospital and now have a much better understanding of what's involved. I imagine that some of you will react strongly to what I'm about to say. But I think I can answer most of your doubts." After giving his audience some 'background notes' on what it's about to hear, Rod goes on to express his point of view.

To remind yourself to prepare the other person for the conversation that follows, you can say things like: "I think it would be helpful if I spent a few moments putting you in the picture" or "Let me fill you in on the situation before we talk in more detail."

Teller Skill 4 Filling in the picture with important points and useful details "There are two reasons why I need to leave early. First of all, I still have some college work to do. I'm stuck with this essay…"

Headlines and underlines are great for introducing and reinforcing topics, issues and themes in your conversations. Putting your partner in the picture can also be very helpful. As the Teller, your next step is to make your main points stand out and support them with some useful detail.

Good Tellers make sure they communicate clearly by including the right balance of ingredients in their conversations. They realise how important it is to fill in the picture with interesting and relevant facts.

If you fail to provide any of your conversational partners with concrete ideas and information, they'll be tempted to fill in the pieces for themselves. And, often enough, their assumptions will be wrong, or at least distorted.

Let's look at some 'recipes' that will help you get your key points across, whether you are telling a story, delivering a message or sharing a point of view.

Developing a story. Stories that involve you personally have four essential ingredients, summed up by the acronym **SAME**:

S Situation
   The setting or background for the story.
A Actions
   What you did or didn't do in the story.
M Mental states
   Feelings, emotions, moods and other states of mind.
E Experiences
   What happened to you; what other people did or didn't do.

Rachel visits Dennis at his flat. She notices he is looking very glum, so she asks: "What's wrong. You look down." Dennis replies: "Oh, I had a bit of a problem at work yesterday."

This doesn't sound very interesting, so she moves on to some other issue. What might have happened if Dennis had started with a headline and then gone on to include all four story ingredients? These are the kind of points he might have introduced into the conversation as it developed:

Headline: "I had some bad news yesterday. I was hoping to get on a training course about computers, but I found out that I'd not been selected."
Situation: "I want to get promoted, but for that to happen I need to become expert at using the internet. So when I learned there was one place left on a course, I applied for it. The trouble is, so did three other people … This was all about three weeks ago, by the way."

Action: "Anyway, yesterday I went in to see my boss to find out what was happening. I explained how keen I was."
Experience: "But he really laid into me, saying that I wasn't ready for promotion. It was clear that he was actually enjoying putting me down."
Mental state: "I was shocked and came pretty close to losing my temper."
Experience: "What should have been a pleasant conversation turned into a major confrontation."
Action: "So I walked out of his office and went straight to the personnel department and handed in my notice."
Mental state: "And now I'm worried sick about what to do next."

Rachel, listening to this story, gets the full impact of Dennis's situation, and replies: "Phew. What started out as an ordinary day turned into a disaster. And now you're really down in the dumps about it." Rachel has received the message loud and clear because Dennis gave her the essential ingredients.

How many times do we tell only half of a story and still expect to be understood? For example, if we fail to talk about our own part in the story – what we did or did not do – we come across as victims at the mercy of other people's behaviour and of the situations in which we find ourselves.

Sometimes, if we fail to include a description of what's going on inside us – our thoughts and feelings – we are leaving out what could be an important part of the story. Again, we shouldn't expect people to be mind-readers.

On the other hand, if our story concentrates too much on feelings, at the expense of other ingredients, we also run the risk of being misunderstood. That's because feelings make sense only when they are connected to the other ingredients of the story.

Ordinarily, feelings don't just come from nowhere. They arise because of what happens to us and because of what we do or don't do. Effective Tellers make the connection clear, rather than talk about feelings in isolation.

Expanding a point of view. A lot of conversations involve talking about points of view – how you see things, what opinions you hold. Your point of view is very obvious to yourself, but not necessarily to someone else. That's why it's important to go beyond simply stating your opinion and into explaining yourself more fully. A useful guide here is **PRE:**

P Point of view
    Your opinion on a subject.
R Reasons
    Why you hold that opinion.
E Examples
    Instances that bring the reason to life.

Let's see how this works by considering Liam's opinion on boarding schools. Here are some of the main points he makes during the dialogue:

Point of view: "I don't like the idea of boarding schools."
Reason 1: "For a start, they have teachers playing the role that parents should be doing."
Example 1: "For instance, if a child gets into trouble, like for bunking off, I think it's the parents' job to sort it out."
Reason 2: "Another thing I don't like is that boarding schools don't prepare children for the real world."
Example 2: "When I was a boarder, I spent too much time with children from the same background as me, so I grew up with a very distorted view of what the world is like."

Whether you agree with Liam or not, you at least understand what's behind his point of view. He has used reasons and examples to bring his point of view into focus.

If you don't make an effort to explain the reasons behind an opinion, it can easily come across as a put-down.

Stating an opinion without any supporting reasons is effectively saying: "I don't respect you enough to be bothered with explaining myself." And as we all know, being treated disrespectfully is the quickest route to an argument.

Spelling out a message.

Many conversations are concerned with giving people messages. It's often a good idea to spell out your message in some detail. Here's a simple formula to help you. You can remember it as **MRI:**

M Message
　State the message as clearly as possible.
R Reasons
　Explain the reasons for giving the message.
I Implications
　Spell out the implications of the message – in other words, how it affects you and other people.

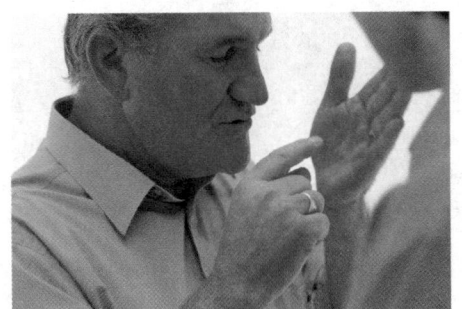

Nick has a message to give his friend about the swimming club they both help to run. Here are some key points he takes care to cover during the conversation:

Message: "I can't come to the committee meeting this evening."
Reason: "My wife's not well, and I have to be with her."
Implication: "The problem is I was due to tell the committee about the arrangements for next week's swimming gala. Obviously, I can't do that if I'm not there. What I'd like to do instead is give you the details, so you can pass them on to the committee. How does that sound to you?"

We tend to be much more detailed and explicit when our messages are complaints or criticisms. So when you want to praise someone, take the trouble to describe their behaviour and its positive effects in specific terms. Consider which of these comments has the most impact:

"Thanks for cleaning up" or "I really appreciate the way you've tidied the kitchen and put all the dishes away in the right place. It was such a relief to come home and see what you had done."

The more concrete, explicit and specific (as opposed to abstract and vague) you are about all the ingredients of your story, message or point of view, the more effective you will be as a communicator. But don't overdo it. Keep in mind the two-way nature of dialogue. Even simple messages are best delivered through dialogue, which allows the other person to check their understanding and contribute their own ideas.

TalkWorks 2

Getting connected **Skills for Understanders** As we've seen, making your points stand out is a vital Teller skill. But what if you are in the role of Understander? How can you make sure you are picking up the right messages, even if the Teller is not being particularly clear? There are two skills involved here. The first is accurately capturing the other person's meaning. The second is feeding this meaning back to the Teller.

Understander Skill 3 Listening for highlights

Conversations tend to be like chocolate chip cookies – a few chips of chocolate embedded in a lot of biscuit. The chips are the Teller's main points. The biscuit is the rest of the conversation – the details that expand on the main ideas, plus all the other bits of chat that glue the conversation together. The Understander has to pick out the essential nuggets of meaning from what the Teller is saying.

Listening is not a mechanical activity like making a tape recording. We need to tune in. We need to concentrate. We need to listen with an open mind. Then, however briefly or automatically, we process what we hear inside our heads as we turn the words and non-verbal signals into meaning.

The quality and usefulness of the Understander's response to the Teller depends on how well this processing is done.

We have already looked at some of the ways that listening can go wrong because of faulty processing. For example, if you listen judgmentally, your processing focuses on the 'rightness' or 'wrongness' of what the Teller is saying – in your opinion – rather than on the intended meaning.

Alice is telling Jim that she is having a baby with her boyfriend. Jim believes very strongly that it's wrong to have children outside marriage. He listens judgmentally and finds that almost everything Alice says is 'wrong'. By concentrating on his own reaction, he misses the point she is trying to make. How can we guard against this trap? This is not to say that Jim has to agree with Alice. Listening well does not mean approving of everything you hear.

The trick is to reflect consciously on what you've heard and convert it into a highlight: a summary to capture an important part of the other person's message. There are often identifiable feelings behind what people say, so it can be useful to include these in the highlight you are capturing.

John spends a couple of minutes telling you a story about his daughter getting into trouble at her youth club. He goes into some detail, but in essence what he's saying is: "I'm worried because she's being bullied and I don't know how to deal with it." That's a highlight. It captures John's main point.

Ernie works in a pub and is talking with one of his 'regulars', Bill. During the conversation, Ernie says: "You've got a family, a kind of back-up to your career. I don't have that. The main thing in my life is my job. It's not that I don't like it. But I've got an itch to do something that'll make me feel better about myself. No, that's not it. I don't feel bad about myself. But I want to do something where I'm using more of my talent."

What are the highlights here? What's important to Ernie? What are the main points he's trying to communicate? How does he feel about things? Asking yourself questions like this can help you capture Ernie's highlights as you build your understanding.

Understander Skill 4 Feeding back the highlights

"So, as far as you're concerned, the local school is ideal for both your kids."

As we've seen, the aim of the Understander is to capture the Teller's highlights. Then what do we do? How do we respond in a way that will help the conversation develop?

One very helpful thing to do is feed back to the Teller some selected highlights. This is useful for two reasons. First, it lets the other person know that you're interested in what he or she is saying and are doing your best to capture their meaning. Second, it enables you to discover whether your understanding is accurate.

Showing you understand. As you listen to Adam talk about his fear of going to the doctor, how can you make sure that he knows you are 'with' him?

There's one sure way. And that's to tell him what you think his main points are. Not just by repeating what he says, of course, but by putting them into your own words. After listening carefully to Adam, you might say: "What worries you the most is simply not knowing what to expect in the future." That's an example of feeding back a highlight.

Carl has been telling you about his views of a particular politician. You have been listening intently and noting highlights. At one point you say: "What you seem to be saying is, he's good at making promises, but when you look at what real changes he's made to the education system, he's achieved nothing."

If you're right, if you've captured the essence of what he's been saying, Carl will tell you. Either directly – "That's right!" – or by continuing with his story, confident that you are with him. He might say: "That's right! Let me give you a couple of examples. Let's take what he promised to do about teachers' pay . . ."

On the other hand, if you're wrong, then the misunderstanding can be cleared up on the spot. Carl might say: "Well, you're right about the promises, but I don't think he's achieved nothing. I can think of quite a few useful things he's done. For instance . . ." You had most of it right. By sharing your highlight, you enable Carl to acknowledge what you'd understood correctly and to amend what didn't quite hit the mark.

It would make for a very strange conversation if you demonstrated your understanding every few seconds. Even so, effective Understanders make a conscious effort to check regularly if their version of the story, message or point of view is the same as the one that the Teller is intending to tell.

The fact is, everyone likes to be understood. It's one of the best feelings we can have. It makes us feel valued and boosts our confidence. It also saves us from having to repeat ourselves because we're assured that the other person is building up the right picture.

Feeding back highlights of the Teller's story, message or point of view is an excellent way to 'lubricate' the conversation so it runs smoothly and effectively.

Put yourself in the shoes of the Teller for a moment. Imagine what it's like when the person you're talking to makes it clear that he or she is on your wavelength and picking up your main points. You feel encouraged. You feel like moving the conversation along.

Here are some guidelines for feeding back highlights when you are in the Understander role:

Concentrate on the most significant thing you've just heard. Keep to the point. Think for a few moments before you speak. Not everything that the Teller says is a highlight. What you're looking for are the main messages.

'Interrupt' the Teller from time to time. If the Teller goes on and on, you'll soon find that you've 'saved up' too many highlights to share. While there are times when it's best to let the Teller have his or her say without interruption, conversations generally go better when there is real dialogue – when both people interact.

Gloria is telling you about some problems she's having with her mother, who tends to be domineering. You say: "Wait a minute. Are you saying that she's often quite bossy, but this time she was actually nasty to you?"

Gloria replies: "Not exactly. I might have made it sound like that. To tell you the truth, I was in a bad mood myself, so what she said probably sounded worse that it really was."

In this case, sharing a highlight helps Gloria tell her story in a more balanced way.

Be concrete and specific in the highlights you share. Don has been talking about how fed up he is with school. You say: "So there are quite a few things you don't like about your school, but what annoys you the most is the attitude of some of the older kids." Don replies: "You've got it. In fact, if the headmaster was a bit tougher on them, I could probably cope with the rest of it."

By feeding back your understanding in your own words, you have put your finger on exactly the point Don is trying to make. This helps him to be clearer in his own mind.

Link feelings to their causes. Generally, feelings are caused by, or accompany, experiences and actions. So, if you include feelings and other mental states in your highlights, connect them to the event or the experience that caused them. Kristin feels bad **because** she was so impatient with her elderly mother yesterday. Allen feels good **because** he's just received a long newsy letter from an old friend.

Eileen is explaining what happened during a conversation she's just had with her sister about plans to move their father into a nursing home. At one point you say: "So you were surprised by your sister's opposition because everything she'd said up to that point indicated she was in favour of the idea." Eileen replies: "Surprised? I was dumbfounded. It was a total about-face."

Feeding back your highlight provides Eileen with the opportunity to make her feelings even clearer.

Acknowledge strong emotions right away. If somebody is experiencing strong emotions, it's often a good idea to recognise this right away in your response. You might say: "That's just the kind of back stabbing that really makes you furious. It's pretty clear you're still steaming over it."

Acknowledging feelings can be particularly important with children, whose emotions are seldom far from the surface. So a father might say to his son: "Jamie, I can see you're upset about being left out of the team. It must seem so unfair to you."

Recognising and naming a child's feelings at the start of a conversation can make all the difference between the conversation going places or it turning into a confrontation. It also helps children to learn to recognise their own feelings and become more confident about putting them into words.

If you're uncertain, check it out.
If you're feeling fuzzy or confused, turn your highlight into a quest for clarity. "Are you saying that your sister was proud of what she did, or didn't really care?" Don't pretend to understand if you don't.

Don't just parrot back what you hear. Nobody wants to listen to a tape recorder. It sounds phony. If you've really understood what has been said, sharing the highlights should sound like you. So use your own words. Don't start sounding like a doctor, lawyer or professional counsellor.

Don't run ahead. Base your highlights on what you've learned so far, not on what you think is coming. Resist the temptation to anticipate people's points and feelings about them. By choosing to feed back highlights, you will automatically become a good listener. That's because your attention will become focused on what the other person is trying to communicate rather than on your own reactions to what you are hearing.

Feeding back highlights will also help you remember the important things that are being said. It's a bit like writing notes to yourself.

How often should you feed back highlights? There is no all-purpose formula here. The idea is to use highlights in a natural way to help the conversation flow and keep your understanding on track.

But there is one simple rule that you can follow all the time: every response you make should indicate in some way that you've been listening and trying to understand.

If your response is a question, for example, the question itself should indicate that you've been listening carefully.

David has been going on about an argument he's had with his brother. Your response might be: "From what you're saying, you have quite a few fights with your brother. What makes this one so special?" The question demonstrates that you have been listening, that you have been identifying highlights, and that you are working hard at understanding.

When you decide to move into the Teller role, again it's very useful to include a highlight in your first remark.

You've been listening to Lawrence giving you his opinion on mobile phones. You might say: "As far as you're concerned, you think they're too expensive for what they offer. Well, for me it's different. I think the expense is really worth it. Let me tell you why . . ."

If people feel they've been properly heard and understood, they are more likely to offer you a similar opportunity to have your say.

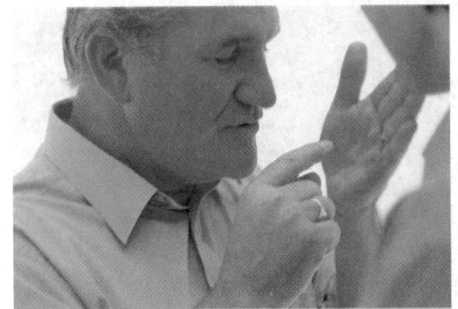

TalkWise
Respecting the conversational rights of others

We all have rights of one kind or another. Under law, for example, we have the right to be innocent until proven guilty. We have conversational rights as well. For example, we have the right to withdraw from a conversation if we believe the other person is behaving too aggressively. Understanding your rights (and the rights of other people) and choosing when to apply them is an important part of being a wise communicator.

Let's take a closer look at our conversational rights. There are times when the purpose and direction of a conversation seems to come from nowhere. It just happens.

This is often the case when people are chatting and wandering from one subject to another. At other times, someone is clearly the Initiator – the person who brings up a topic.

Sometimes the Initiator requires the other person to be the Teller. This is what happens in an interrogation. The police investigator says to the suspect: "Tell me everything about your movements from noon yesterday." In a more friendly setting, Agatha says to her friend Abigail: "Tell me all about your trip – every last detail! I can't wait to hear all about it."

On other occasions, the Initiator deliberately sets himself or herself up as the Teller, and the other person as the Understander, at least for the first part of the conversation. For example, Gary starts off by saying: "I've been on this diet, but I just can't stick to it. I want to tell you about the problems I'm having." Later on, you might become the Initiator/Teller as you bring in another subject – for example, your own difficulties with trying to stay fit.

Have you ever found yourself in a conversation you wished you weren't having? Of course, you have. Sometimes it's because you are a reluctant Initiator. A father, for example, might not enjoy having a conversation with his son about his rudeness to a teacher. In this case, the son might also want to avoid the conversation. Nevertheless, it takes place, because the matter needs to be dealt with.

But there are other times when it's better to exercise your right **not** to initiate a conversation, even though there might be some good reasons for doing so. For instance, it might help Victor to hear some feedback on his embarrassing behaviour at the party last night. But you choose not to give it. You have a feeling that the conversation would only aggravate the problems you're having between you. And in any case, you don't think it would make any difference to Victor's behaviour.

You also have conversational rights when the other person is the Initiator. There are times when it makes better sense not to engage in a conversation started by someone else. Here are a few circumstances where this could happen:

The moment is wrong. You might be preoccupied with something else that needs to be done or you're in the wrong frame of mind. You could be very tired, for example. If you explain this openly to your conversational partners, they'll often see it as a mark of respect rather than rejection.

There isn't enough time. You might only have a few minutes, and you feel the conversation deserves more time than that. If you are rushed, you won't listen very well. So you might say: "I've got to leave for a doctor's appointment in about ten minutes. We need more time. Can we talk later?"

The situation isn't right. You might expect to be constantly interrupted – by the telephone, for instance. If you're willing to try, then the best solution is to explain the situation and leave the decision to the other person. This is the respectful thing to do.

The subject is out of bounds. For example, the other person might want to talk negatively about someone who's not there to speak for herself. If this makes you uncomfortable, say so. That's your privilege.

One useful idea, when faced with a problematic situation, is to agree a conversational 'contract' with the other person. Explain what you think it's okay to talk about and how much time you have. For instance, you might say: "I'd really like to hear about this, but I have to go in 20 minutes and I'm expecting a friend to telephone any moment now. We might not be able to finish. Is that all right with you?"

Staying on course **Skills for Tellers and Understanders**

Now that we've looked at some core communication skills, we're ready to think about some additional skills that will make your conversations work even better. On the Teller side, we'll be discussing ways to give your stories and messages impact and colour. On the Understander side, we'll be considering ways of responding that lead to fuller understanding and avoid damaging the conversation.

Teller Skill 5 Bringing your story to life "This job is just so amazing. I'm already responsible for the new line of perfume – and they're sending me on a marketing course two days a week."

When we looked at the Teller skill of 'filling in the picture', we considered formulas that can help you include the right kind of ingredients in your conversations. We're now going to look at how to bring your points to life so that your stories, messages and views have impact and colour.

One of the keys is to make your details **concrete** and **specific**, as opposed to vague and general.

Take a few moments to imagine a building . . . it's almost impossible, because the word 'building' is too general to picture.

Now imagine a thatched cottage in the country, surrounded by pretty gardens and bathed in sunlight. That's much easier to picture, because the description is specific. It has the kind of detail that helps the Understander to visualise what you are saying.

Conversations that create pictures in the other person's mind, or offer some other form of clarity, usually have far more impact and are easier to share. Consider the difference between these two statements:

Version A "I've been let down by her. It just didn't work out like I expected."

Version B "I've been betrayed by someone I really trusted until I discovered she'd been playing a game with me all along. I'd pour out my problems to her – I thought in confidence – but then she'd go and talk about me behind my back."

The first is a statement of fact, but it lacks life. The second contains the sort of detail that gives life to the facts. It helps the other person to 'connect' with what's being said.

Don't forget that you can also communicate through your non-verbal behaviour. If you are genuine and mean what you say, this will help ensure that your body language and voice quality reflect your spoken messages. If you are not a naturally expressive person, try to be more conscious about using your voice and gestures to add emphasis to what you are saying.

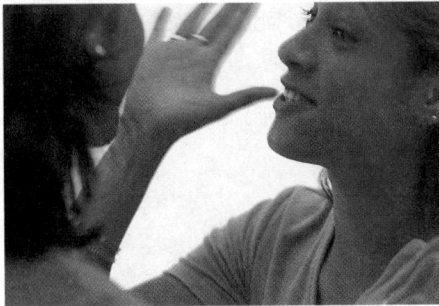

There are various ways of making a **story** more compelling. For instance, when telling a story about yourself, become the 'leading actor' in your story. Put yourself centre stage. Re-live the incident as you talk. Recall the sights and sounds, the thoughts and feelings just as they were at the time.

Nina is looking for a new job. She's talking to Lionel about a recent interview she's had. She wants to tell him about the interview with a view to getting his thoughts on how she might do better next time. She says: "Overall, I think it went quite well. But I could be fooling myself."

The problem with this description is that it doesn't give Lionel any real sense of Nina's experience. There's not enough meat on the bones. So he finds it difficult to be helpful.

Nina has another go. This time, she says: "When the interviewer asked me what I found most difficult in my present job, I realised he wanted to know something about my 'weak spots', the things I don't do that well. My heart pounded a bit, but I thought I could take something that sounded negative and turn it into a plus. So I began by saying how I'm sometimes too hard on myself and too soft on others. I tend to find fault even with the things I do well. On the other hand, I sometimes find it difficult to tell people off when their work is sloppy. He seemed to take it on board, but I'm not sure if it made him think the better or worse of me."

In this version, Nina brings her story to life. This gives Lionel something to work with. The two of them go on to discuss the best points in her 'interviewee' style and ways she might improve.

There are ways of bringing your **messages** to life, making them clear and forceful, without overwhelming the other person. Remember the **MRI** formula. Add zest and punch by 'humanising' the reasons behind the message and the implications it holds. Here's Zoë telling a friend about a decision she's made:

"I've decided to sell my car and not replace it. I imagine this sounds a bit crazy, but I have thought about it. I'm keen to actually do something about the environment, rather than just talk about it. And to be honest, it's going to save me quite a lot of money, which is what I need to do right now. It means I'm going to have to change my lifestyle – use the buses more often, maybe cycle to work. And it could mean I'll be begging a lift off you now and then."

There are ways of sharing a **point of view** with conviction, and even passion, without giving the other person the impression that you are trying to ram it down their throat.

Harriet is talking with her husband, Nathan, about her elderly father. Nathan has suggested that Harriet is not paying enough attention to her father's needs. Harriet shares her point of view on this subject.

She says: "I love him. Well, he is my father after all. But that doesn't mean he's perfect or that I should overlook his faults. I think he's much more self-centred and controlling than he might appear to you. He admires you and tends to be very reasonable when you're around. But he constantly manipulates me – or at least tries to. I get so annoyed. I know this sounds harsh, and I don't want to overstate my case, but take last year's holiday for instance. He pressured me for weeks to invite him along, and look what happened – he was miserable the entire time and it spoiled the holiday for the rest of us."

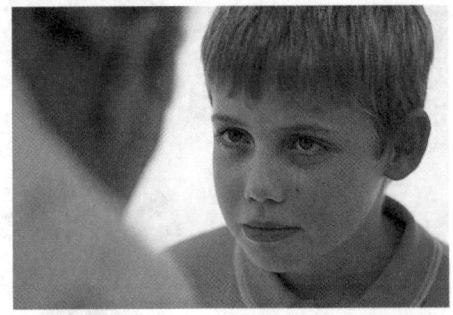

Harriet moves beyond the bare facts. She shares her view about her father, is open about her feelings and uses a specific example to bring her point to life.

Bringing your story, message or point of view to life does not necessarily mean lots of words. Effective communicators don't go on and on with irrelevant detail. Think about someone telling a joke well. He or she gives you only the details necessary for the punchline to have impact. Too many facts get in the way. The idea is to say what's necessary and helpful and then encourage the give-and-take of dialogue.

If you feel you're cluttering the other person's mind with too many details, take care to place special emphasis on your central point: "I guess the most important thing is . . ."

Teller Skill 6 Using self-disclosure to personalise your communication "Look, I've made mistakes too. I still regret not putting more effort into saving my marriage."

One of the prime purposes of conversation is to establish, deepen and maintain relationships. Intimate relationships that are enjoyable, productive and lasting can only develop when people know each other beyond a superficial level.

But what does it mean to 'know' another person? It means knowing something about what he or she thinks, feels, believes in, worries about, hopes for. It means knowing something about the experiences that have helped shape his or her life.

Many conversations are directly or indirectly about getting to know each other better. Interestingly, talking openly about ourselves not only helps other people to get to know us. It can also help us to know ourselves a little better. It's amazing how often we gain a clearer idea of what we really think and feel as we put them into words for other people.

Many of the most rewarding relationships in life – those that involve helping, coaching, teaching, supporting and encouraging – are impossible without openness. A teacher can't help a student unless the student is open about what he's finding difficult. A father can't help his teenage daughter deal with a problem unless she gets the problem out in the open.

Self-disclosure and intimacy tend to go hand in hand. Intimacy can exist in many different settings – within families, between friends and at work. Intimacy usually involves some kind of balanced exchange of personal details. (Nobody likes people who only listen and never reveal anything about themselves – or people who're only interested in talking about themselves and aren't interested in learning about others.)

Building relationships through being open does not mean 'letting it all hang out'. The key skill here is making sure that what you reveal is appropriate to the situation. Think of it as exchanging gifts.

The trick is to make sure the 'gift' of personal detail is right for the occasion. Disclosing too much personal detail can make the other person feel uncomfortable and shut the conversation down.

Different kinds of intimacy are nourished by different kinds of openness. For example, the intimacy between people who work together can be highly rewarding but is very different from the intimacy that exists within a family.

When Alice reveals to her co-worker Roger that she's frightened of negotiating deals with big customers, this is an important thing to reveal. The fact that Roger knows almost nothing about Alice's personal life is irrelevant to their relationship at work.

Here are some of the ways you can use self-disclosure to personalise your communication:

Telling stories about yourself or incidents that have had significant impact on you. Some of the delights of Gerry's early years were the vivid and often hilarious stories his mother told about her family and friends back in the little town where she was born. At the time, Gerry had no idea how important this was in 'getting to know' his mother.

When Hilary told Betty about the lingering pain she feels about not being able to have a child, the two women become even closer friends. Betty took the self-disclosure as a sign that Hilary trusted her deeply.

Sharing points of view about significant issues in life. Adrian never really knew his friend Liz until she shared some of her religious beliefs. These beliefs were a key to many of Liz's behaviours – both her kindness and her sticking to principle. Understanding the source of these behaviours helped Adrian to appreciate his friend even more.

There is something deeply comforting about realising that other people have also been through similar experiences to yourself and that your thoughts and feelings (while very much your own) are not unique in themselves.

Talking about yourself endlessly, is, of course, boring to others. On the other hand, sharing some of your thoughts, feelings, opinions and history can add both clarity and zest to your conversations and your relationships.

Understander Skill 5 Working to get the full picture
"Well, I can see why he was disappointed, but I really
don't understand why he actually fired her."

Good Understanders play an active role in ensuring that they acquire a thorough understanding of the other person's story, message or point of view. They are never satisfied with partial or fuzzy understanding. Instead, they accept responsibility and take positive steps to gain a fuller, clearer picture.

There are two main things you can do to assist the Teller to be clear and complete. The first is to make remarks that encourage the Teller to carry on 'telling'. The second is to 'probe' for additional information by asking helpful questions. There are two issues here. One is making sure you seek out the right kind of information. The other is making sure the Teller understands what it is you want to know about.

Some Tellers do better when they are actively encouraged, especially at the beginning of a conversation. There are a number of ways you can stimulate the flow of any conversation:

Respond with interest. Like newly born babies, conversations can be at their most vulnerable during the first few moments of life. So make sure your first responses are actively encouraging. For example, you might say such things as: "That sounds important to you" or "I'd like to know more about this."

Your non-verbal behaviour also tells the other person a great deal about your interest – so remember to make eye contact.

Use prompts. Drop in the occasional remark that demonstrates you're listening and involved. Interjections such as "uh-huh" or "I see" can act like injections of encouragement – provided they are genuine.

As we've learned, feeding back highlights is a wonderful way to motivate the Teller. But it's not always necessary to share a complete chunk of understanding. A few words will often nudge the conversation on. For instance, if someone is telling you how she's been let down by a friend at college, you can encourage the flow simply by dropping in a few of words like: "And you really trusted him". It shows you're tuned in.

Leave room. Don't feel compelled to fill in all the conversational spaces. Sometimes, it's a good idea to give the other person time to gather his or her thoughts. Staying silent for a few moments may be all that's needed, provided you've demonstrated your initial interest. But don't overdo it. If the silence drags on, the Teller might feel like he or she is being put on the spot.

Don't assume that any of your conversational partners will automatically know you are interested in them. If you don't make your interest clear through words and body language, they may decide that you are closed to communication – especially if they're feeling insecure about the conversation in the first place.

As you try to build your understanding, there will be times when you need more information to fill in a story, clarify a message or understand a point of view.

This does not necessarily mean the Teller is doing a poor job. It means that you are taking responsibility for your own understanding, no matter what kind of job the Teller is doing.

The first step is to work out what it is you want to know. Go for the most important missing pieces rather than detail for the sake of detail. The **SAME**, **MRI** and **PRE** frameworks are useful guides.

If the Teller's **story** is not clear to you – or is not as full as you'd like – use **SAME** as a kind of checklist. Ask yourself questions like this:

Situation: What more do I need to know about the background to the story?
Actions: Do I understand what the Teller actually did or didn't do?
Mental state: Am I clear about the Teller's feelings and what is behind them?
Experiences: Do I know enough about what other people did in the story?

For example, you might ask for more information on Experiences and Mental states: "So what happened after Mary walked out of the classroom . . . and how did you feel about it?"

If you're unclear or confused by the Teller's **message**, remember **MRI** and ask yourself questions like this:

Message: Have I understood the real message being expressed? Is she saying one thing, but meaning another? Does her body language confirm or contradict her words?
Reasons: Do I understand the reasons behind the message? If a friend tells you about a change in plans, for example, you might ask: "So what led you to change your mind?"
Implications: Am I clear about the implications of the message for me, and anyone else who might be affected? You might ask: "Does this mean I have to change my plans as well?"

If you're struggling to be clear about someone's **point of view**, think about **PRE** and ask yourself:

Point of view: Do I really understand their point of view? How strongly does the other person hold this view? Is it a big issue, or relatively unimportant?
Reasons: How much do I know about the reasons behind the view?
Examples: What examples would help me understand better?

Good communicators automatically ask themselves questions like these in order to build their understanding on firm foundations.

Questions need to be handled with care. They can sometimes be a barrier to communication rather than an aid to understanding. For example, some questions limit the conversation by containing their own answer. These are the type of questions heard in courtroom dramas: "Mr Smith, exactly when was it that you first decided to steal the statue?"

Other types of question to avoid are those which set out to 'trap' the other person. For example if you ask someone: "What are you doing tomorrow night?" it's only fair to reveal your reason for asking. It's more honest to say: "I'd like to find out if you could look after the children tomorrow night."

Our daily conversations are packed with questions. In fact, questions spill out of our mouths with ease. Yet not all questions are equally helpful in our search for better understanding.

The most effective are 'open' questions – ones that can't be answered with a simple "yes" or "no". Open questions tend to develop the conversation. Questions that can be answered with a "yes" or "no" are much less effective and tend to close the conversation down.

Closed questions. Lily and Serena have been talking about Serena's problem with a local builder who did a bad job on her roof but is still demanding full payment for the work. Serena explains that she's sent the builder a heavy letter. Lily asks: "Did he reply?" Serena answers: "Not really." The conversation isn't getting very far. Lily tries again and asks: "You mean you didn't get the response you wanted?" Serena replies: "That's right." The conversation is getting stuck.

The problem with closed questions is that they tend to generate more closed questions. And too many questions in a row can soon make people feel under attack, as if they're in an interrogation rather than a conversation.

Open questions. This time Lily asks: "What did the builder do after he got your letter?" This question can't be answered with a yes or no. Serena replies: "Well, I got this message on my answering machine. But he didn't say much, other than accuse me of over-reacting. I get the feeling he's unwilling to put anything on paper in case I take legal action." The conversation has moved on.

Open questions (which often begin with How, Who, What, Where, When or Why) leave the responsibility for filling in the picture with the Teller, which is where it belongs. Think of questions as 'openings' you offer the Teller – or as hooks to draw out information essential to your understanding.

As well as searching for information through direct questions, you can build your understanding through indirect questions. These can be very powerful for opening up conversations. Here are some ways you can ask them:

Offer a topic. Simply invite the person to talk, without making it into a question. Just say what it is you'd like to hear about. "Tell me about your first day at work." A request like this leaves the field open to the Teller.

Explain what you want to know. State clearly what it is you want to find out about. If it's helpful, also explain why you want to know it. "What I'd like to know is how the argument started, because I still don't understand why the two of you couldn't agree." Another example: "I can see why you think A levels are perhaps not right for you, but I don't have much idea of what you'd like to do instead."

Build on what you've learned so far. Ask the person to expand on what's already been said. Put yourself in the request to show you're personally interested and involved. "You've said some people got angry. I'd like to know the kind of things they were saying."

Search for clarity. Use comments that emphasise your own lack of clarity. For instance, when you hear somebody half-saying something, you might say: "You said John sometimes behaves irresponsibly. I'm not sure what you mean by 'sometimes'."

Ask for examples. If someone is expressing a point of view but it isn't yet clear, you might ask for an example. "If I'm understanding you right, you believe that the local council is letting the town down badly. Can you give me an example of what you mean?" When asking for examples, be careful not to make it sound like you're really saying: "I don't believe a word of what you're telling me!"

Voice your thoughts. It can be helpful to let the other person know what's going on in your mind as you listen. For example: "As I hear you describe Ken's family situation, I realise how little I know about his parents."

Work hard to gain clarity in your own mind. Encourage people to be precise and concrete. If you are puzzled, say so and ask for clarification. This is the work of the true Understander. "I still haven't got the full picture. I'm still not certain exactly what it is you'd like me to do."

It's important, however, not to go overboard in your search for clarity. Remember that you're looking for the main pieces, not seeking detailed evidence for use in a courtroom.

Skilled Understanders keep conversations alive by using a mix of responses – prompts, encouraging remarks, highlights, open questions and indirect questions.

Whatever response you make to the Teller, the aim should always be the same – to demonstrate, check and build your understanding. If your response does none of these things, then you are not playing the role of Understander to the full.

Imagine you go to see a doctor. You begin to tell her about your situation. What you want is for her to listen and encourage you to talk fully and openly before discussing the recommended treatment. But instead, she responds in one of these ways:

She writes out a prescription before you've had the chance to explain yourself properly.

She criticises you for being ill – for not taking care of yourself in the first place.

She dismisses your illness as trivial, even before you describe what you believe to be the main symptoms.

She offers you some pills she's taking herself.

She starts to talk about the state of her own health.

If you had this experience, you'd probably think about changing your doctor. None of her responses contributes to the creation of a satisfactory conversation. They all take the conversation off-course and all have the power to destroy it. Yet responses like this are very common in our everyday conversations. As we look at some examples, see how familiar they are to you.

Giving unwanted advice. Many of us are too fond of offering instant advice. Trevor is listening to Alistair talk about a dispute he's having with Sandra at work. After a couple of minutes, Trevor says: "Get rid of her! She's trying to take over, you know, get your job." How can Trevor's advice be useful if he doesn't know the full story? So before you even think about offering advice, build your understanding.

The truth is that we often give advice when it's not even required. Does Alistair really want Trevor's input? Perhaps all he wants to do is share his thinking. If Trevor acts simply as a sounding board, Alistair may well come up with his own solution to the situation, and the solutions people think up for themselves are usually the best ones.

So, rather than offering instant advice, concentrate on helping people find their own answers instead.

Judging. Too often, without realising it, our responses can come across as judgements and criticisms. This happens especially if we have been listening from a right/wrong perspective rather than with an open mind. We can be judgmental in both direct and indirect ways.

Responses that attack or demean the other person as an individual are direct judgements. They almost always have a negative effect. Trevor says: "Come on, Alistair. Your problem is you're just too soft."

Some judgmental responses are indirect. Questions are often judgements in disguise, as these examples show. "Why did you do that?" often really means "I don't think that was the right thing to do." "Were you actually surprised?" often really means "Surely you must have seen it coming." "Do you think you should have done that?" often really means "What a stupid thing to do."

While these questions might look innocent on the printed page, in practice they are often asked in a way that makes their real meaning, their judgmental meaning, quite clear. Often it's the tone of voice. "Why did you do that?" is asked in an I'm-better-than-you tone that turns it into a clear criticism.

Dismissing. Dismissing another person's point of view or feelings as unimportant is the same as dismissing the person. William is talking to Harry about how he missed out on a new job. When Harry says: "Forget it! It's not that important!" he is devaluing both the problem and its owner. An effective Understander would have fed back a highlight and perhaps asked for more information. He or she might have said: "I can see you're upset. I'd like to know why this new job was so important for you."

Hijacking. Another response to avoid is the 'hijack'. It's very common but highly irritating and unproductive. Here's how it looks from the Teller's angle. You're in the middle of telling a story when the other person picks up on something you've said and instantly uses it to take over the conversation.

Ramesh is talking to Jon about a problem with his girlfriend. He says: "We were on a camping trip, so a lot of what happened took place in the middle of the countryside..." Jon cuts in: "We used to go camping ourselves. In fact, we're thinking about doing it in Scotland this summer..." Jon has hijacked the conversation away from Ramesh, before he'd had the chance to make his point.

Some hijacks are deliberate, but most are done unconsciously, often as a result of either self-centred or half-hearted listening.

If you decide that you have to hijack a conversation for some reason – for example, you may think of something important that can't wait to be said – then take responsibility for putting the conversation back on track.

Josephine interrupts: "Excuse me, but listening to you talk about your car made me remember that I've forgotten to book mine into the garage. Let me jot down a reminder to myself." Josephine writes herself a note. She then returns to the conversation: "Now, you were talking about how unreliable your new car is ..."

This is just common courtesy. Most of us hijack conversations (or seriously drift off the subject) far more often than we realise. See if you can catch yourself and others doing it.

In a fun conversation, say a chat in a pub, hijacking makes little difference. At other times, however, it undermines or destroys the conversational climate. The message delivered by the hijack is: "What you're saying is not important to me."

TalkWise
Making feelings and emotions serve your conversations

We all know that feelings and emotions are part of the fabric of our conversations. So let's consider what we can do to use emotions to set and maintain the right climate for dialogue.

We're all familiar with the saying: "Sticks and stones may break my bones, but words will never harm me." Well, that's nonsense. Words can harm us in many different ways. In fact, the usual distinction between 'words' and 'actions' doesn't hold true in many cases. Words often are actions. Soothing words for a person in physical or psychological pain can sometimes be better than any pill. Words spoken in anger, on the other hand, can have the impact of a sledgehammer.

There are things you can do (and refrain from doing) in both the Teller and the Understander role to make emotions friends rather than enemies of dialogue.

The starting point is this: we can control our emotions and make them serve our relationships more than we realise. It's all too easy to 'blame' our emotions for our actions. This is just another way of avoiding responsibility for our own behaviour. "He made me angry, so I told him what an idiot he is. We haven't talked since." If we don't remain in charge of our emotions, they will quickly take charge of us.

In his book 'Emotional Intelligence', Daniel Goleman put together the case for emotional self-control. Here's a summary of his suggestions:

Get to know your own emotional patterns: "I tend to blow up easily when I'm challenged."

Learn how to manage them: "I realise that Evelyn always rubs me up the wrong way, so I need to be particularly careful when I'm around her."

Use emotions to motivate yourself: "I feel really positive, so I'll have that talk with Fela I've been putting off."

Recognise other people's emotional patterns: "Eddie is easily hurt when his efforts aren't recognised."

Handle your own and other people's feelings and emotions as part of managing relationships: "My tendency to fly off the handle combined with Anne's thin skin is an explosion waiting to happen. I need to read her reactions carefully and keep a check on myself."

Expressing negative emotions freely does not have the benefits some people think. Often enough, giving vent to anger makes us only more angry. This does not mean we should become emotionally 'neutral' or bland. That would rob life of its colour. There are times when we should express anger. The issue is how to express it.

Connor and Alice wanted to have at least three children, but ended up with a single child, Melanie. This has become a source of tension in their marriage and they often disagree about how Melanie should be brought up. They have been talking about some problems Melanie is having at school with her classmates.

During the conversation Connor says heatedly: "You're just too protective. You can't wrap her in cotton wool and pretend other children don't exist. You can't arrange her life so that nothing ever goes wrong. It's unfair to her. I think you're jealous about any relationship she has. Maybe even about her relationship with me."

As soon as I saw you, I thought 'Bunny Rabbit Pullover'.

I feel really irritated when salesmen are over friendly.

As often happens when people get angry, Connor says more than he means. He exaggerates to make his point. In the process he says some hurtful things.

So what is Alice to do? She might retaliate, which could turn the conversation into a battle. Or she might become defensive, in which case she might try to change the topic of the conversation or even end it. In either case, the conversation fails to develop and important things are left unsaid.

Alice chooses neither of these options. Instead, she pauses a bit, then says: "I know you're angry . . . We've never really come to grips with not being able to have more children and how it's affected us. It's probably time we did. The point you're making is that I haven't handled my share of the problem very well. Well, that's fair enough. But I also think that we need to talk about what we've been doing jointly as parents."

Instead of accusing Connor of being unfair or criticising him in retaliation, Alice is open about her own responsibilities and suggests that it would be good for both of them to have a dialogue they have been putting off. Her emotional control clearly helps the conversation to make progress.

Emotional control at the service of dialogue can be exercised in both the Teller and Understander role. This doesn't mean we must only have 'nice' conversations. There will always be times when you need to say things other people might not want to hear. But if you anticipate how they may feel as a result, you can do your best to make your point in a way that still recognises and respects their feelings.

There's a lot of difference between speaking in anger and speaking about your anger.

Home sweet home. A lot of arguments, particularly within families, are sparked off by remarks that attack or belittle the other person – either directly ("Don't be so stupid") or indirectly through sarcasm, mockery, ridicule and any of the other ways we 'get at' people.

Here's a typical situation. Barry has promised to get tickets to a pop concert for himself and his sister Gail but has forgotten to do it. When Gail finds out, she lashes out at him: "You really are selfish, you know that? You knew how much I wanted to go the concert and now you tell me you can't get the tickets in time. Can't you ever think of anyone but yourself?"

Faced with a comment like this, the temptation is to react instantly with a cutting remark of your own. So Barry says: "Me? Selfish? What about you? You're always the one who decides which TV programme we have to watch." And they're off into a family squabble that leaves them both in a bad mood – and does nothing to solve the ticket problem.

What Barry could do instead is to buy some breathing space – just a few seconds is usually enough – to allow his own emotions to calm down. Then he'll be more in control of himself. So instead of reacting right away, he concentrates on the message behind his sister's outburst and considers the 'truth' of what she is saying. To show his sister he's been listening and understanding, he feeds back a highlight – and adds a "sorry" because in his calmer state he's decided that he owes her an apology. Using this approach, Barry says: "I can see why you're having a go at me. That's fair enough, because I let you down. I'm sorry. Let's talk about what I can do to fix the situation."

If you're on the receiving end of a wounding remark, you always have a choice. You can allow yourself to be hijacked by your own emotions or you can let the attack go by and wait until your emotions have settled down before responding in a more level-headed way.

Now look at the same conversation from Gail's side. She also has a choice. She could have waited a few seconds before making her opening remark, again to allow her temper to cool. This would have made it easier for her to make her point without turning it into a personal attack. This time she simply says: "I'm mad at you for not getting the tickets. I was really looking forward to the concert." She's made her point, but avoided sparking off a family feud. A good rule here is: 'attack the problem, not the person'.

I forgot that Gloria gets annoyed when I question her too much.

I need to remember that Jack gets angry when I challenge his point of view.

Moving on Skills for Tellers and Understanders

The skills in this section can help put the finishing touch to conversations. On the Teller's side, we'll look at the idea of actively checking to see whether the main points of your story, message or point of view have come across. Another Teller skill we'll consider is how to invite the other person into the dialogue. On the Understander's side, we have two more skills to talk about. One is using summaries to double-check your understanding. The other is concerned with switching to the Teller role when this adds value to the dialogue.

Teller Skill 7 Summarising and checking for clarity with the Understander "So, just to make it absolutely clear, let me run over the main points again."

A good way to promote full understanding is to summarise your main points every once in a while. The idea is to pull all the threads of the conversation together in order to emphasise the key points.

Lucy has been talking for over ten minutes with Winston about their company's new sales brochure. She summarises: "Let me see if we're on the same wavelength about this. I want the brochure printed by the end of the month. I think it should have photographs of all our new products. However, you think there could be a problem with the timing, because the photographer isn't available for another week. Is that how you see it?" Winston replies: "That's about it. You know, maybe I should look around for another photographer..."

If the message being delivered has important implications, then summaries are almost essential.

Luther and Kirstin are having a good dialogue about their plans for a holiday. At one point, Luther volunteers a summary. He says: "If I've got this right, we both want a holiday in the sun, but your main concern is to go before the crowds arrive. That probably means June rather than July or August. And we'd both like to have your mother come along, but she still isn't sure if she can take the time off work." Kirstin responds: "That's how I see it too. We'll have to find out the deadline for making final arrangements and let my mother know. If she can make it, great. If not, we can do something together later in the year."

Of course, not all conversations sound as idyllic as this. But you get the point. Well-placed summaries in conversations can add both clarity and impact.

How do you know if someone is 'taking on board' what you're saying? There are two things you can do. One is to be alert for signals which indicate that you are 'losing' the other person. The other is to check directly to see if your points are 'getting through'.

Looking for non-verbal clues.

As every comedian and public speaker knows, an audience can provide all sorts of clues about how well the performance is going down. If people are shifting around in their seats, for example, this could mean that the performer is 'losing' the audience. After reading this signal, the experienced performer might say to himself: "My timing seems to be off. Perhaps I need to speed up a bit."

Good communicators, when in the Teller role, also look for clues in the other person's reaction to what's being said. One valuable source of information is body language – everything from facial expressions to hand movements and posture.

Here are a few of the most common 'warning' signals that tell you if you're losing the other person's attention:

**Eyes wandering
Fiddling with things
Shuffling feet
A secret glance at a watch
Slumping posture**

When you see one of these signs, it may be time to ask yourself what you can do to get your point across more effectively. Or it may just be that you've turned the conversation into a one-way speech that excludes the other person. In that case, stop and invite the other person in.

Listening to verbal clues. You can learn a lot about how well you are being understood by listening carefully to the other person's responses. So as well as working hard to get your point across, make sure you remain sensitive to what the other person is saying back to you. An 'off-target' question on the other's part, for example, can alert you to a potential misunderstanding.

If your conversational partner appears to be misunderstanding you, try to be patient. Control the impulse to blame the other person. Instead, accept responsibility for their lack of understanding and try to get your central point across once again. For instance, you can say something like: "I guess the point I'm trying to make is . . ."

Checking directly. The surest way to discover if someone is getting your message is to check directly. You can say things like: "I'm not sure if I've made myself clear. I'd like to know what you've picked up from what I've said."

Jack is a teacher. After giving Richard instructions on a science project, he says: "I'd like to know if all this is making sense to you. Perhaps you could go over the instructions for me." Richard replies: "I think so. Basically, you want me to connect the motor to the transformer and then see how much faster the motor turns as I increase the voltage."

Caroline has been discussing travel arrangements with her daughter Claire. She says: "I appreciate this is all a bit complicated. Could you just go over the details for me so I know we're clear about things." Claire replies: "Okay. You want me to pick up the clothes from the dry cleaners, then go to the station, where I have to wait at the ticket office for Dad, who should arrive about 4 o'clock."

A huge amount of misunderstanding, frustration and wasted effort could be eliminated from our lives if we developed the habit of checking that the other person really has understood what we've been saying.

There are many different ways of inviting the other person to feed back their understanding. However you do it, the point is to convince yourself that the other person really has received the message you've been aiming to get across.

Teller Skill 8 Bringing in the Understander "Well, that's how I see the plan working out. Now I'd like to hear your views on the subject."

As we discussed right at the beginning, conversations work best when they are true dialogues – when both people share the work of building understanding by responding to each other and exchanging ideas.

Sometimes this happens naturally. People take turns, switching from Teller to Understander and back to Teller as the conversation progresses. The conversation feels like a shared experience. At the end of it, both people feel satisfied, even if the subject being discussed is potentially touchy.

There are other times, however, when it's a good idea to make a conscious decision to switch from being in the Teller role to the Understander role. Or, to put it another way, to invite the Understander to become the Teller – the person who's now leading the conversation.

Suppose you've been telling Ida the **story** of your driving test – how nervous you were, what happened when you got caught in a traffic jam, how you thought you'd failed but were thrilled to discover you had passed. To bring Ida into the dialogue, you could open the door by saying: "I'd like to know if anything similar has happened to you."

Imagine you've been giving your brother a **message** about your decision to work abroad. You've taken care to explain your reasons for moving and how this might affect things. For instance, in the future you won't be able to play such a large role in looking after your mother.

You can make sure your brother participates fully in the discussion by deliberately requesting a response. You might say something along these lines: "I'm wondering what you think about all this. It'd be great if you could come up with any ideas on how I can help with Mum, even though I'll be out of the country."

Picture a conversation where you've been expressing your **point of view** about re-decorating the house you share with your partner. You've explained your preference for wooden floors, given some reasons and backed them up with an example or two. You recognise, however, that your partner has just as much interest in the house, so you issue a clear invitation by saying: "I've had my say, and thanks for listening. I'd really like to find out what you think."

The main point is this. Don't always wait for other people to take on the role of Teller. Invite people in throughout the conversation, without necessarily waiting until you've had your full say. Take care to let them know their contribution is valued.

Understander Skill 7 Summarising for complete clarity

"Let me see if I've got this right. There seem to be two main reasons why you want to move house."

From the Understander's point of view, checking understanding is a fundamental part of the role. As we've seen, you can do this throughout a conversation by feeding back highlights to make sure you are staying on track.

Some conversations can get quite complicated. In this case it can be useful to take a break from time to time in order to check back with the Teller.

The idea is to pull the main points together and replay them as a summary to the Teller to see if both of you are in agreement on what's been communicated.

As well as providing the Teller with the opportunity to correct you or change the emphasis, summarising also helps you, the Understander, to get the ideas straight in your own mind. Summarising what you've learned, in your own words, is a proven way to embed things in your memory.

Alexis has been talking with her father about changing her course at college. After several minutes of discussion, her father says: "I'd like to see if I've heard you right. It seems that you want to change from doing chemistry to business studies. But this means you'll have to stay at college for an extra year, assuming the college will allow you to switch. You're also worried how your Mum and I will feel about all this, because it may involve us in extra expense."

If the father's summary is accurate, this provides a good platform for a further dialogue about the issues involved.

Summaries are also a useful way of moving a conversation along. If you find the other person is rambling or giving too much detail, combine a summary with a request for more information. This is polite way of saying: "I've got it! Let's move on."

Christopher and Lucinda have been talking for quite a while about a car boot sale they are helping to set up. Christopher has made the same point several times. So Lucinda finally says: "From what you're saying, you think we might have a problem getting enough people to turn up. As you've said, there are several other events happening over the same weekend. Let's talk about what we can do to make our sale a success."

Understander Skill 8 Moving into the Teller role to add value to the dialogue "I like your ideas for the party, though I do have a few concerns. Let me give you some of my own suggestions."

Knowing when and how to switch from Understander to Teller is one of the great skills of successful dialogue. Sometimes you make the switch in order to help the other person – for example, by telling someone about your own experiences in a similar situation.

At other times, you switch in order to make sure your own needs are met – for instance, by responding to a message that affects you in some way. Let's see how this can work in practice:

Ahmed is trying to come up with a plan that will enable him to earn a living while studying at college. He left school when he was sixteen but now wants to further his education. He feels his lack of qualifications is holding him back. His friend Sue wants to help. She's happy to have a conversation around Ahmed's issue.

During the early part of the conversation, Sue stays firmly in the role of Understander. Her initial job, as she sees it, is to help Ahmed express his ideas and be clear in his own mind. So she tunes in and encourages the flow by prompting him from time to time.

As the conversation develops, she feeds back some highlights so that Ahmed knows she is with him. She asks some direct and indirect questions to fill in the picture. Now and then, she summarises to make sure her understanding is on target. She does her best to avoid offering instant advice or criticising.

Is this all she can do as she tries to help Ahmed? Must she stay in the Understander role throughout the conversation? Of course not. Sue can also help by sharing some of her own experiences and points of view that relate to Ahmed's issue. When she does this, Sue moves naturally into the Teller role – but still with the aim of supporting her friend.

At one point, Ahmed says: "I guess what I'm most concerned about is whether I'll be able to cope. If I take on too much work, I could mess up at college. But on the other hand, I need the money from a job to survive."

Moving into the Teller role, Sue says: "I think I had a taste of that. For a period I worked nearly every night while I was finishing off my nurse's training during the day. I could just about handle it. But I had no other life. In the end I got through okay."

Ahmed says: "I'm not so worried about college. I'm sure I'm going to enjoy that side of things, but I'm still anxious about fitting everything in."

Sue says: "Well, one thing that really helped me was getting the right job. I started off working in a bar but then switched over to doing babysitting. The pay wasn't so good, but it gave me more time to read my textbooks, which took a lot of pressure off me."

Ahmed finds Sue's account of her own struggle very helpful. It gives him encouragement and some ideas he might otherwise not have had. The conversation continues, with Sue sharing more of her experiences and points of view, but always making sure they are relevant to the conversation's purpose.

Knowing when to switch from Understander to Teller is never more critical, perhaps, than in conversations where two people are exchanging opposing points of view.

Tom and Alan are talking about their very different views on racial discrimination. Conversations like this often turn into arguments and confrontations very easily, with both sides trying to 'win' at the other's expense. There is another way.

Tom listens to Alan. Instead of instantly challenging Alan with his own competing point of view, Tom controls himself and stays in the Understander role for several minutes, even though he's bursting to disagree.

Rather than trying to cut Alan off, Tom gives him the space to make his point. Tom sticks at it until he's confident that he understands Alan's view. He then demonstrates his understanding by summarising as accurately as he can, but without feeling he has to agree or disagree. Tom says: "What you seem to be saying is, racism has always existed and always will, so there's nothing we can do about it."

Alan is satisfied that he's been listened to respectfully. At this point, Tom says something like: "You know, I have a different way of looking at things." He then goes on to explain his own point of view. Alan now gives Tom the chance to express himself clearly. After all, that's only fair because Tom gave him his undivided attention.

At the end of the conversation, they both feel valued, heard and understood – and perhaps discover that their differences aren't so great after all.

To sum up. Instead of trampling over other people's points of view, concentrate instead on understanding them as best you can. Once you've achieved this, you have earned the right to have your own views heard and understood.

While it sounds easy on paper, this kind of conversation is difficult at first for many people. We are so used to having confrontational conversations (verbal 'sword fights') that we find it hard to hold back and let other people have their say.

TalkWise
Reading and responding to situations

When you enter a conversation, there's usually something already going on in the background. Richard may be preoccupied with tomorrow's exam. Nick and Fiona, two friends you're having a drink with, are clearly frosty towards each other. Perhaps they've just had an argument. Robert is low because he's recently heard that his sister is seriously ill.

So before you get yourself into a conversation, it often pays to pause and ask yourself: "What's going on here?" By reading the situation, you'll be in a much better position to make the conversation work well.

Many conversations fail simply because they take place at the wrong time or under the wrong circumstances.

Terry is in the middle of his homework, concentrating on an essay he has to finish that night. His mother interrupts and starts to talk about the untidy state of his room. Is Terry in the right frame of mind to listen?

Anne is seething with frustration because she's lost her purse and credit cards. Her partner picks that very moment to begin a conversation about their plans for the weekend. Is Anne in the right mood for that kind of discussion?

A group of friends are chatting about this and that. The mood is light. They just want to have fun. Is this the right time for you to start a conversation about a mutual friend who's just told you she's getting divorced?

If you suspect the time and place might be wrong, ask the other person if it's okay to talk.

This is a particularly good idea when you telephone someone, because of course you can't see what's going on at the other end of the line. It's a sign of respect. It also gives the other person some options. He or she could say: "I'm in the middle of something right now. Let me call you back in an hour or so."

Listening in to your shadow conversation. How many times have you finished a conversation with someone and then later on wished you'd said more of the things that were on your mind at the time? On the other hand, how often have you said something and then later regretted it?

Knowing what to include (or exclude) from a conversation can be tricky, but we do have a useful tool to help us make thoughtful decisions. It's called the 'shadow' conversation.

When two people are talking, there are actually three conversations going on. There's the external conversation. And then there are the internal or 'shadow' conversations that go on privately inside each person's head. In other words, during a conversation, we not only talk to each other, we also talk to ourselves.

The trick is to be aware of your own shadow conversation but without becoming too preoccupied with it. If that happens, you can't really listen to the other person. On the other hand, it's worth eavesdropping on your shadow conversation because some of the things you say to yourself can usefully be brought out into the open.

Trish is having a meeting with Albert. During the conversation she says to herself: "He might not realise it, but he's being a bully towards me." But she says nothing. While driving home, she says to herself: "Once again, I let him play the bully with me. Unless I speak out at the time, he'll keep on treating me like that." The next time it happens, it might be best for Trish to voice her thoughts out loud as they occur to her.

Dorothy is talking with Grace about an exhibition of local artists they are helping to organise. Grace hasn't been doing her share of the work. She's been missing deadlines and often letting people down. During the conversation, Dorothy says to herself: "I've got to find a way to confront her about this."

Later in the conversation, Grace reveals that her husband has recently lost his job. Dorothy says to herself: "This is definitely not the best moment to discuss it. But it has to be done sometime soon." Dorothy is wise to listen to her inner voice and keep her thoughts to herself – at least for the moment.

Of course, some thoughts will always need to stay private. They might be hurtful or offensive if brought out into the open. Or they might be irrelevant to the conversation at hand. There are no cast iron rules to guide you in how you can use your shadow conversation to best effect. But here are a few tips:

Be aware. Stay in touch with your inner voice.

Keep your self-control. Don't get distracted by it.

Check for relevance. Remember the purpose of the conversation.

Be sensitive. Choose carefully what you move into the external conversation.

Be courageous. Have the guts to say things that will help.

Putting it all together. The final part of the book pulls all the skills together and explains how you can use them to 'fix' conversations that aren't going well. We also look at the idea of a communication 'style'. Like everyone else, you already have a communication style – a 'typical' way of interacting with people that reflects your existing skills and attitudes. The great thing is that you can develop and enhance your existing style – and as a result enjoy better conversations – by absorbing the TalkWorks approach into your normal way of communicating.

How to maintain and repair conversations

Imagine for a moment that you are running a meeting. There are eight people sitting around a table discussing how to organise a charity fun run. It's your job, as the chairperson, to make the meeting work as well as possible. From time to time you intervene. You notice that Mukesh hasn't said anything for a while, so you invite him to join in. You realise that Karen has gone off the point and so you politely remind her what the meeting is all about.

All in all, your aim is to make sure the meeting runs smoothly and gets fixed if it stops working for some reason.

You can do the same with your own conversations. You can take on the task of maintaining and repairing dialogue. But with one big difference. The person whose performance you are monitoring is you, whether you're in the role of Teller or Understander.

We all make mistakes in our conversations. Even the most skilled people sometimes get it wrong. They let their emotions get the better of them. They run into a lazy spell and don't use the skills they have. They get carried away and forget the other person. But all is not lost. If you're aware of what's going on, your inner voice may well say something like: "Look out. Marsha's getting agitated because you're not giving her the chance to speak." Or: "I've just been very sarcastic to Dan and he's feeling under attack. I'd better repair the damage right away."

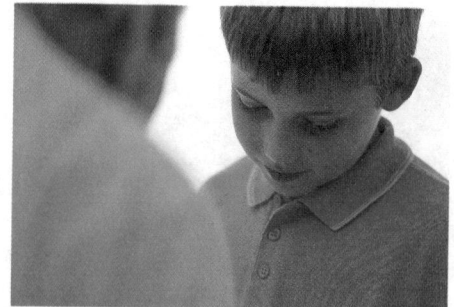

There are two ways of repairing a conversation. One is to do it privately. That is, by working within the conversation itself. For example, you realise that Hilary is confused by what you're saying. She's frowning perhaps, and clearly not getting your point. Realising that your story has become disjointed you decide that the best way to get the conversation back in shape is by giving Hilary a short but precise summary of the story so far. Hilary now gets the point. The conversation is repaired.

Here's another example of a private repair job. Liam is telling you about his adventure in France. You realise that you've drifted away and have lost the plot of his story. So you consciously re-focus your attention and work hard to pick up the story.

You can also repair conversations publicly. That is, by being open about your mistake and having a mini-conversation to get the main conversation back on track. Here's how it can work:

Adam is talking to Lanny about his stressful lifestyle and how it is damaging his health. Lanny, in the meantime, is thinking about his own situation. He suddenly realises that he's not heard a word of what Adam's been saying for quite a while.

At this point, Lanny says: "Adam, could we stop for a moment? To tell the truth, I haven't been listening very well. As you were talking about being stressed out, I started to think about my own anxieties. I'm sorry about that. I'd really like to hear what you've been saying, so can you put me in the picture again."

In effect, what Lanny does is take a 'time out' from the main conversation to make the repair.

Let's look at another example. Faye is talking with George about her weekend. She realises that George is beginning to look bored. The conversation has been one-sided and she sees that she's not been picking up cues that George wants more interaction. She stops and says: "Good grief! I've been going on and on. I've even seen you start to say something and then interrupted you. Just steamrolling along. I apologise, George. I really want to talk with you rather than at you. Tell me about your weekend." Faye has put the balance back into the conversation, moving into the Understander role.

Conversational repair demands vigilance. Look out for signs that the conversation isn't working. Listen to your shadow conversation. If you find yourself saying things like: "Oh, she's beginning to get impatient", decide how to repair the situation. Can you do it privately, from within the conversation? Or is it best to take a break, apologise openly and get the conversation going again?

Helping the other person play

Life would be much easier if everyone you came into contact with was a skilled communicator. But that's not the case, of course. So what can you do when you find yourself in a conversation with someone who doesn't know how to 'play'?

If you have the skills needed for conversational repair, then you also have the skills needed to help other people to do a better job as both Understander and Teller. This needs to be done without being patronising or condescending because the "I'm smart and you're not" attitude destroys the very foundation of dialogue.

Helping the other person to be a better Teller. Suppose the other person's story, message or point of view is muddled, vague or lifeless? The question is – what can you do to help him or her become a more effective Teller?

For instance, what if Lucien is rambling? Rambling is a mixture of things. In Lucien's case, the problem started when he failed to put you in the picture or give you a headline. You have little idea of what the conversation is about. Also, he doesn't give you enough detail to work with. What's more, he's telling his story without any personal angle.

Any one of these problems is a possible opening for you to make a helpful suggestion. Essentially, what you want to say is in the spirit of: "This is what I'm experiencing as I try to understand you. Here's how you might help me do better." Notice that you are not accusing the other person, but are asking for their help. Here are some of the things you might say to Lucien:

Background: "Hold on a minute, Lucien. I'm getting bits and pieces of the story, but I have no idea how it all started. I'm a bit lost. It might help if you gave me some more of the background to all this."

Purpose: "Lucien, I need to know something. Is this conversation related to planning the holiday or is it about something else? I'm confused because we said we'd sort out the holiday this evening."

Clarity: "I know you went to the travel agent's office, but I'm not sure what actually happened there. Perhaps you could give me a few more details."

Message: "Lucien, you've given me lots of information, but I'm not sure I get what's behind it. It would help if you could tell me what your main point is."

Helping the other person to be a better Understander. Suppose you're in the Teller role and you find that the other person isn't performing very well as an Understander. You might find that your partner isn't listening with an open mind, isn't picking up the right points or feeding them back to you, isn't exploring for a fuller understanding by asking useful questions.

What can you do to help him or her perform better as the Understander? The trick is to encourage the other person to do things you try to do when you're in the Understander role. As before, what you want to say is along the lines of: "This is what I'm experiencing as I try to tell my story, message or point of view. Here's how you might help me do better."

Indira is talking with Emily about a plan to put on a charity supper at the village hall. As Indira talks, Emily does little other than nod her head now and again. But when Indira stops talking, even briefly, Emily cuts in and makes her own point.

What she says has little connection with what Indira's been saying. It's as if she hasn't been listening. Indira realises what is happening, so she begins to help Emily play a more partner-like role in the dialogue. Here are some of the things she does:

When Emily fails to feed back any of her understanding, Indira says: "I'm not sure if I'm explaining myself very well because I don't know what you think about my suggestions so far. I'd really like it if you could give me some feedback."

When Emily jumps straight into a new idea, without referring to what's already been said, Indira says: "I'm getting confused. I find we're jumping around from one idea to another a bit too fast for me to cope. I'd find it helpful if we could deal with one thing at a time."

In short, without being patronising or condescending, Indira helps Emily to play a fuller and more effective role as the Understander.

What's your communication style?

Like everyone else, you have your own distinctive communication 'style'. It is made up of the characteristic ways in which you communicate with other people. You probably have an overall style, and a variety of sub-styles for different settings. For instance, your style at work or school might be quite different from your style at parties or at home.

Here are a few descriptions that indicate what is meant by style:

"John tends to ramble when he's explaining things, and I find myself switching off after a few minutes. This means that I miss a lot of what he says."

"Martina asks too many questions – it's like being interrogated by a detective rather than having a conversation. I wish she would just listen to me once in a while."

"Tony seems to listen to people. But when he talks, what he says is hardly ever connected to what the other person has been saying."

The first comment is about John's Teller style. The second is about Martina's Understander style. The third is about Tony's failure to engage in dialogue.

Most of us have a mixture of strengths and weaknesses. We are good at some communication skills, but not so good at others. For instance, Tina has this to say about Larry:

"Larry is a very good listener. He's a great person to talk to when you are trying to sort out a problem. His sincerity comes through in just about every word and gesture. But he shares practically nothing about himself. There's just not enough give and take for real friendship."

It's important to realise that your style is not something you inherit. It's not fixed. You can, within reason, develop the style you want. Here's what someone says about Michael's positive communication style:

"I enjoy being with Michael. I've never said this to him, but he brings out the best in me. There is so much interaction in our conversations. And there is such variety, too. We can just mess around. We can be serious. We can talk about his problems or mine. We can even talk about how we relate to each other. Sometimes I wonder what kind of communicator I am, but when I'm with Michael, it all seems so easy."

What's your Teller style like? What's your Understander style like? What kind of 'dialoguer' are you?

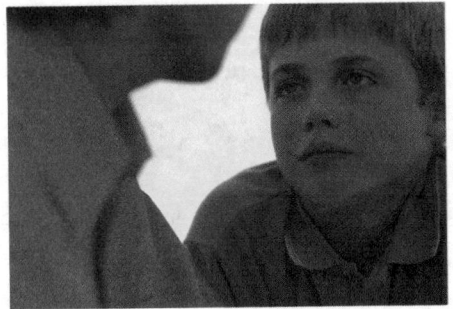

What's your reputation?

Your communication style gives rise to your 'reputation' as a communicator. Your reputation is based on how particular individuals experience your style over a period of time. Your reputation is important because it can have a huge influence on the way other people interact with you.

In a sense, your reputation precedes you in every conversation you have with people who know you well. Before a word is spoken, your own reputation will have created a set of expectations in the other person's mind.

For instance, Dan thinks of Samantha as someone who tends to criticise him a lot, and this affects the way he relates to her. In particular, he is unwilling to be open with her about his problems because he doesn't want to subject himself to a stream of criticism.

With some people, Andrew has a reputation for letting his emotions get the better of him. He takes offence easily and sulks when his views are challenged. As a result, people tend to leave him out of discussions because few of them want to deal with his over-sensitivity.

Do you know what your own communication reputation is among the people who matter to you? It may be exactly what you think it is, or it may be altogether different.

Your reputation may vary quite widely from person to person. Someone may be an excellent listener to her daughter, for instance, but not so good when dealing with a certain colleague at work. A man might talk easily about himself to his mates in a pub, but find it difficult to be open with his wife.

A simple way to find out about your reputation is to ask. Seeing ourselves as others see us is not always a flattering experience. But it's an important step towards changing. So pluck up the courage and ask a few of your friends, family and colleagues what they think about you as a communicator. Ask them what it feels like to have a conversation with you. This will help you decide which of the skills described in TalkWorks are the ones for you to concentrate on first.

No one is a perfect communicator. We can all improve and become more consistent. As we said at the beginning of this book, virtually every aspect of our lives depends on communication. So if we can improve the quality of our conversations, we can expect to see the quality of our lives – and of those around us – to improve as well.

Free Communication Style questionnaires. To help you evaluate your own communication style, we've developed a special pack containing five questionnaires – one for you to fill in about yourself, and four for other people to fill in about you.

To order your free questionnaire pack call **Free***fone* **0800 800 808.**

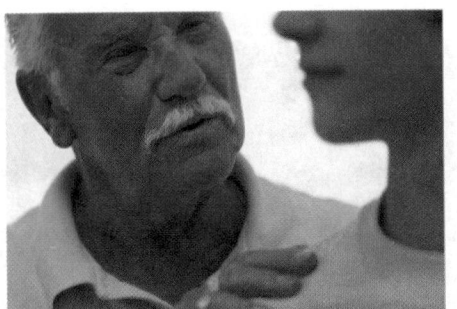

HISTORY: TalkWorks is a current product produced initially as part of BT's Millennium Programme known as FutureTalk. It still forms the basis for all of BT's educational communication skills materials and is currently being expanded to include collaboration as an example of 'Dialogue in action'. There are a number of other products in the series related to communication skills which can be viewed on the websites below. There may be a small charge for the adult materials, but all the education materials are FREE. TalkWorks remains an OCN (Open College Network) accredited course

NOTE: This remains a current BT publication

Contact: Better World Campaign, Goonhilly Visitor Centre, Helston, Cornwall, TR12 6LQ

E-mail: bt.betterworld-resource@bt.com

Telephone: 01872 325588

Websites: www.numberoneskill.com
                 www.btbetterworld.com